The First  of Genesis

of Genesis

*a fresh approach to
an ancient story*

Book One in the Series:
Life Coaching Genesis

Phillip L. Ball

THE FIRST 77 WORDS
OF GENESIS

*A FRESH APPROACH
TO AN ANCIENT STORY*

BOOK ONE IN THE SERIES:
LIFE COACHING GENESIS

PHILLIP L. BALL

© Copyright filed June 2022 by Phillip L. Ball

Phillip L Ball
   9207 S. 43rd West Ave.
   Tulsa, Oklahoma 74132-3714
   philball@cox.net

    This book is the first in a planned series of books giving fresh perspective on the amazing stories in the Bible's book of Genesis.

    The second book in the series will address the second account of creation and the life issues and perspectives I reimagine from the story of the *first humans*, their *perfect* life in the garden and the choices related to becoming fully human with all its gifts and challenges.

    Stay tuned!

DEDICATIONS

This is the part of the book I usually skip when I open a new book.   It's OK if you're like me. Skip it.

What seems important to me is that I bear witness in print to the reality that none of us show up knowing very much about anything without having had tremendous help that extends far beyond anything we might have either planned, earned, or deserve. These few words are my attempt to recognize and honor some of those Spirits and people.

Mary Ruth Scoggins Ball, my grandmother born in Cherokee County, Georgia in 1874. She was a kick ass female person whose spiritual sensitivity and perception passed through my father to both my older brother and myself. She was a distance empath who even when a child I recognized we had a spirit connection that was never spoken about. My spirit recognized her power and I was honestly a little leery of getting to close to her. She died when I was 10.

Only as an adult reading a family story written by one of her daughters about her *powers* did I make sense of our family's spiritual heritage. Then later with my Aunt Ruth, her youngest daughter, I would experience the empathic sensitivity first hand. That knowledge helped me understand more about myself so that I might be more in harmony with my own true nature and it's origin.

My mother Thelma Ball for reading stories to me about stories in the Bible.

The people of Centenary Methodist Church who provided an emotionally healthy loving environment in which I could grow, expand, be safe, and be claimed by God's spirit.

The United Methodist Church whose structures educated me, and nurtured the many men and women who loved me and others, offering many new possibilities for growth, expansion, and inclusion even before they knew how important it would become later in life.

Martin Luther and John Wesley who allowed scripture to transform their lives.

The 1952 Episcopal Book of Common Prayer and its obsessively overwhelming list of Psalms and Lessons for the Christian Year that served as a road map to the most powerful stories of our faith.

All the people who had to endure my sermons while I was figuring out how to sort through *1900 years of interpretation, ideas, concepts, tradition, and disagreement* regarding scripture and its interpretation before I could filter out what seemed most important.

The people of First Christian Church [Disciples of Christ], Tulsa, who chose the [United Methodist] Abingdon Press: *Becoming Disciples Through Bible Study,* and the men and women who wrote the study which I had the assignment to teach for 8 years. It's structure, authenticity, and order was very influential in furthering my development.

Professor Manfred Hoffman my seminary faculty guidance counselor who told me truth and spoke with grace.

Chaplin Charles Gerkin [Head Chaplin of Emory University Hospital and later, Professor of Pastoral Care at Candler SOT] whose honesty and insight regarding spiritual and emotional gifts I had yet to realize led me one step closer to understanding myself as a perceptive and compassionate person God might use in a helpful way.

Jerry Ball, my big brother whose steady insight and presence gave me a safe place to rest when I allowed myself to be pushed beyond all my resources.

Diana Ball who married me and whose love God used to saved my life.

My Daughter Allynn Young whose amazing presence taught me to claim and love the child in myself as I was inspired to care for and love her.

ACKNOWLEDGMENTS

I feel called to **acknowledge** these **spirits and people** who have been essential to the production of this book.

The living **Spirit of the Holy Divine Creator Source of the Universe** [like in "everything"] who is at once beyond the scope of my greatest imagination, and at the very same time the most personal intimate healthy parent father/mother/friend that one could imagine. Without Her leadership and inspiration I wouldn't exist. Without His vision, prompting, and ever present *spirit leadership* this project and all those yet to be written would never see words on pages. Thank you! What a great trip!

Diana who *always loves me, and desires the best for me. What a great gift treasure!*

Allynn who can sense and see where I am going with my writing while understanding what I am attempting to accomplish, and who then offers imagination and perspective to both my presentation and style adding significant value to it. Our dialogue has vastly improved the focus and clarity of my work.

Lynn Q whose willingness to read and correct my grammar, punctuation, WILD CAPITALIZATION, **continual over bolding** as well as my ever present *italicization* has calmed me down and taught me more grammar than I was previously willing to learn. And still there are occasions I have chosen to ignore her best efforts. Thank you Lynn!

Professor Robert Alter who from the age of 15 began to be captivated by the Hebrew language, and who has been dedicated to the effort to translate the Hebrew Bible into English.

While he does not know I exist, I have a strong sense of who he is. I have watched videos of his presentations, listened to the style and tone of his voice, gathered in the subtle objectivity yet genuine sensitivity with which he both shares and simultaneously limits his opinions to provide space for the reader/listener to form his/her own conclusions. *I can feel* what I sense in him is the authentic spiritual presence of those ancient people who received and told the stories for a thousand years before they were reduced to writing.

Professor Alter has been free to share his studied sense of the best the English language can do in revealing the most authentic meaning from a written Hebrew translation.

The most I can say is THANK YOU PROFESSOR ALTER! Your work has allowed the living sense of spirit, message, and meaning from those ancient spiritual forebears to come alive for me.

PROLOGUE

IF YOU WILL READ THIS the rest of the book will give you its gifts more easily.   Thank you!

    Because I am writing this prologue after having finished the content of my book, it may bring a special gift. Like a good map it may be able to show you a way to realize where you are in the forest of words as your read.

I was given Brene Brown's new book *Atlas of the Heart* for my 77th birthday this year. In her introduction she offers the *metaphor of mapmaking* as a helpful way to approach the research she has done in constructing her *atlas* of human emotions a reader might explore and discover. We all know how challenging it can be when attempting to sort through and gain perspective on the layered, confusing, complex, and many times contradictory *feelings we experience* in our lives.

    Brene's idea was to make an Atlas, you know, like *Rand McNally's highway Atlas for 2022*, only it was an *Atlas* of the multitude of emotions we humans experience. Before she began she decided she should get educational help in *map making*, and called her friend Dr. Kirk Goldsberry, a mapmaker and a cartography scholar from the University of Texas at Austin. She discovered maps were made in layers with many criteria dependent on the purpose of the map. Is it a map of roads, elevation and terrain characteristics, weather and rainfall amounts, or what? I use printed maps in many ways and had never considered the versatility of a map or the importance of maps in our lives. *My new awareness struck a chord in what I needed to share* about the book you are about to read.

The map of this book comes in two layers. Part One is an educational layer in which I describe using a *compass of questions* to ask of any Biblical text. It then flows into *5 key aspects of awareness* that serve to unlock critical approaches of reading the Bible that are outside common sense reading habits. Part One concludes with two final points leading you to consider *the characteristics of the Bible's oral tradition* and then an effort to *set you up* to encounter the first creation story in Genesis

Part Two is a model of how I actually DO what I have described in Part One. I personally read and experience the first 77 words of Genesis from the stand point of a Life Coach. I take a personal journey down the road of *reading and discovering meaning in my life from the text of the first 77 words of Professor Alter's translation of the Bible's book of Genesis.*

All of this comes from a teaching model I learned in 1970 from educators in the United Methodist Church. *Learn about it, teach it in a practical way, and then do it yourself in the manner you described when teaching while allowing others to experience the results of what you taught. Then encourage them to use similar patterns in their own encounter with the material at hand.*

I hope this process will be helpful if you decide to read additional chapters and verses in the Hebrew scriptures [Old Testament] for yourself.

*Life Coaching
the*

The First 77 Words of Genesis

A fresh approach to an ancient story

by Phillip L. Ball

**Book One from the Series
"Life Coaching the Book of Genesis"**

~INTRODUCTION~

Let me be the first to welcome you as you read this story about *Spiritual value and meaning* from the first 77 words of Genesis. I'm excited for you to join me in this journey of exploration, and hope you find in it gifts for your life.

This book's origin comes from my life-long *adventure in discovering meaning* from this *library of literature* gathered into one large collection called the **Holy Bible**. In my professional experience it seems that people hold the Bible in reverence, put it in places of honor, and rarely read it. Over years of learning, living with, and teaching the stories of the Bible my appreciation and amazement at the wonder I felt in the manner in which the first story tellers portrayed the Spirit of God, the human experience and the journey that is life while attending Planet Earth University has grown beyond comprehension.

Here's my attempt *to care for you* as you consider going further into this book and the Bible.

You may find this book to be helpful...
 If 1) You have ever attempted to read the Bible only to find yourself frustrated or *lost* after a few sentences seeming to tell a story that is totally out of touch with common knowledge of modern science; **if 2)** You are in the process of deconstructing your unsatisfactory religious story in the attempt to reconstruct a more authentic meaningful relationship you could **own** that connects your unique spirit to God's unique story; **if 3)** You had a spiritual experience and find yourself on a spirit quest, and thought *it would be a good idea to check out* **the BOOK** which serves as a foundational document for three of the world's major religions; **if 4)** you have an *important person of influence* in your life with strong viewpoints and opinions about the meaning and purpose of the Bible's message which you find unacceptable; **if 5)** you have heard much about the Bible, seen it in sitting around in the homes of your friends, discovered a copy in every motel room in the United States, took a *required* introductory course in a school or college associated with a religious movement, *and wonder, "What the hell?"*; **if 6)** you've tried enough, lived enough, suffered enough, and had a few "*come to Jesus moments*", stimulating you to think, "*maybe it's time to figure out some shit for myself?";* **or finally, 7) if** you find yourself longing for an authentic **source** that might allow you to access a **Life-giving Creator Spirit** which might provide you with a touchstone of meaning *within all being,* your time spent with the Bible may offer you a wonderful access point.

My goal is to increase your education, your perception, your approach and your development of life-giving resources through your encounter with the Bible's story. In an *auto mechanic* metaphor, I want you to have more useful tools in your Spirit tool box. Working on your car with the help of only a *'moncky' wrench* and a hammer will leave you frustrated and the automobile broken and bruised. This book offers effective flexible tools!

In this book: **A)** *I will offer an educated informed and honest perspective on how to approach the Bible with understanding, and making sense of it in an **authentic and personal way**.* **B)** I will not even **attempt** to tell you what you SHOULD believe or do. *[Life Coaches have no place in telling anyone what they should or should not believe or do!]* I will tell you some questions to ask of the text, and **what I have personally discovered for *my* life in that process of exploration through *inquiry*. C)** In *part 1 of the book* I will teach you about the Bible's origins, and tell you a story about it in hopes you might understand more of the Bible's "Narrative D.N.A.". Once you identify its **story telling D.N.A. you can ask the story questions of meaning, and apply that process to any part of the Bible**. That is what I model in *part 2* of the book. As I model the process, I look at the first 77 words of Genesis chapter 1 and respond to it with questions which reveal understanding and applications for my life as a real person who is attending *Earth University*. **D)** I will teach you how to read and ask questions of the text through a process that I use to discover meaning in my life and personal experience. **E)** I will offer contrasting ideas and opinions to help make sense of some religious doctrine and/or dogma as I feel the need. **F)** I will reveal how AMAZING the Bible is as a **work of art** in literature that can continue to reveal its secrets and perceptions as long as the reader continues to question, grow, and evolve spiritually, intellectually and emotionally within themselves. **The Bible is an organic piece of art with a seemingly magical ability to tell your story and mine as we are willing to allow!**

I have witnessed people attempting to read the Bible as if it were a *shop manual* describing how to *assemble a good life* by following a list of rules, or a *history book* reporting factual information about humanities' ancient past while describing God's exact behavior. **That is a very restricted, limiting, historically conditioned approach**. I have great compassion for people wanting to discover quick meaning and simple answers. Life is complex and difficult. Surprises abound! Challenges arise with each day's sunrise. Even with the best religious incantation of liturgy, holy words, or sacred ritual, God's Spirit remains abstract, unmanipulatable, and generally unrecognized or discovered through the scientific method of inquiry.   In the last 200 years in the U.S.A. I believe that in order to make *religious sales* -*called evangelism*- professional Christians have reduced, simplified, and limited the scope of the Bible's message to discernible *cultural behaviors* defining what is *unacceptable* rather than attitudes and behaviors that are in harmony with the expansive grace of God's Spirit.

I offer you a chance to discover what intelligent dedicated scholars who lived with the text of the Bible every day for much of their adult lives have come to understand through their studies. It is presented with as much certainty as can be applied to a document like the Hebrew Bible [called the Old Testament] that was pieced together over a span of 200 years [between 400 BCE and 200 BCE] with other pieces added as late as 200 of the Common Era [AD]. ***The Bible tells stories*** *within the setting of history so people might discover the nature of God, their own humanity, the nature of life lived in community, as well as a life lived in relationship with* **both** *God and our fellow humans all mixed together.*

> **PRAYER TIME:**
> In my experience I have found that prayer at the start of my day, or prayer before I have a coaching session with a client - *the client will never know* - generally makes things more productive or helpful in all ways. I have decided to interrupt your reading here in the early stages of this book to offer a prayer for you as the reader. You may find more **PRAYER TIME** boxes as you read.
>
> ***Wonderful Creator:*** *Into your presence we are crazy and bold enough to arrive on this day. We come bringing some of who we are in hopes that your amazing Spirit might wrap your hand around our shoulders with one arm, and raise a pointed finger off into the horizon with a vision of what we might do, become, and learn along the Way of this day. We have picked up this book to hopefully learn something important about You, Your Way, our special unique spirit, and the gifts you placed deep within our beings when we were born. We move forward not knowing what we don't know, but we are still moving forward. We seek your help without knowing exactly what help we need. What we do know is that we are here now with you. Thank you for being here now with us. Amen.*

As you read, you may *suddenly realize* **the Bible is in most respects the opposite of a well constructed novel.** It is disconnected from both analytical thought and a scientific world view. The story line may be proceeding in a coherent fashion only to be suddenly interrupted by a new narrative that doesn't appear to be related. Maybe it's something like traveling along a big city street which suddenly changes names without any apparent reason. *[I learned about that while negotiating the streets in and around Atlanta, GA.]* The Bible's stories originated beyond 3000 years ago in a collection of mythologies constructed to help people live in a world they didn't understand, didn't control, and in which they wanted to stay alive. You will come upon illogical twists and turns that seem to lead nowhere, and stories in which the main character acts with an absence of ethical guidance betraying a loved one in order to save his own life only to have things *magically work out* because of the divine intervention of a personally involved caring God Source. Hang on and pay attention!

The Bible is a very difficult piece of literature from which to learn because it seems to REQUIRE that we GET INTIMATELY INVOLVED WITH IT. A helpful comparison that comes to mind is from considering qualities of *a **serious romantic relationship**.* If we are to discover real value in a romantic relationship *-or any other serious friendship-* **we have to get to know one another**. We have to **desire** that relationship. In it we will learn things we don't currently know. We will play and dance with the stories like we do a wonderful partner, and we will fuss and fight when things seem to take a turn in a direction we neither understand nor want to go. I have found that process far more rewarding than one might initially expect. **It is worth the effort!**

There are people *who are not willing* to make the investment in **either** *romance* **or** *reading and discovering the Spirit of God in the stories of the Bible.* That's OK!! No JUDGEMENT! It's finally **your life to be lived**.

Author's Note:
This is the first of my **Author's Notes**. I have decided to stop your reading from time to time in the attempt to help you gain perspective. Before we move forward I want you to allow space for the awareness that **part 1** of this book might feel a bit challenging to read. This book is written with the intention of **both** *teaching* you how to read the Bible, **and then** in **part 2**, *demonstrating what **my reading the Bible** in the way I am attempting to teach has **revealed to me for my life's understanding**.* This *style-attitude-approach* may **require pacing yourself**. The implications are for *both this book and the Bible:* please **pace yourself**. As my father once proclaimed when I left the house in a hurry during my teenage years, *"Take your time while you hurry!"*

I started slowing down and pacing myself with the stories of the Bible as I began creating sermons that could be relevant to the lives of the people in my congregations. I didn't know it at the time, but *that was*

> **one of the primary characteristics of my reading the Bible that gave me time and space to realize relevant connections in my life and the lives of others.** It seems that retention studies are true: We retain 90% of information we teach, and only 5% of what we hear in a lecture.

I've been in a long term love affair with the Biblical text since I was in the 4th grade. My mother was responsible for that, but that's a story for another day. After college, and marriage, and finishing seminary, and two children, and 3 years as an associate pastor in a large church in an urban setting, I was assigned as the *lead pastor* for the United Methodist Churches in two small rural communities in central Oklahoma. I was 28. Because I had to preach twice each Sunday, and chose to follow a prescribed set of lectionary texts, I began to pay very close attention to scripture. For the next 10 years as a preaching minister *I rode the scripture discovery pony* for all it was worth. I learned and learned. I was so moved from that experience that later in my professional career I became the primary teacher for youth and adults in the study of the Bible in a large downtown congregation of the Christian Church *[Disciples of Christ]*.

I want you to know this about me: I am a very honest practical person who has a low tolerance for ideas and platitudes that fail to function in a helpful practical way in my -or another person's- real *no B.S. life*. I bring **THAT compass of value** to everything I do. Truth being told, I also want you to know before we go any further that *I am a living anomaly* as a preacher/minister. I do not fit cultural stereotypes or expectations. I am not a religious salesperson (evangelist) because I don't trust salespeople. Their job is to sell. The **details** that elevate something from *"good enough for government work"* to *"that is the most superb example of craftsmanship I have ever seen"* are the guiding values in my life and work. My job is to educate, nurture, and reveal. If something is not useful for the advancement of a human life well lived on Planet Earth I'm not very interested. That's why in retirement I became trained as a Life Coach.

As a Life Coach exploring scripture, my goal is to explore and integrate the Bible's stories in the real, human, messy, conflicted, and contradicted reality that is a life being lived in Earth form. I am driven by my passion to understand and embrace the *Spirit-of-the-Holy-Divine-Creator-Source* that is woven in, around, through, and under every story in Genesis because I experience it in my life as a tremendous asset - even the stories that first appear as being a little *nuts* to the mind of people reading it as one might respond to a modern news report or novel. Scripture is not "a report" of anything! ***It is a story of constant discovery.***

Author's Note: As I stated above, this book is broadly divided into **two sections**. The **first** is my attempt to teach you **how to read or approach** the scriptures in a manner that allows them to reveal their wisdom. If you find yourself needing something more/sooner in order to keep your attention, **I recommend skipping to page 19** where you can begin the **second half** of the book. You may discover **you then have questions about what led me to interpret or make meaning** of the text in the way I did. If that is the case please **return to part 1,** and discover the process that led me to the interpretations I share. If none of this works for you then, Thank You for giving it a chance!

I start with Genesis because it is a collection of amazing stories having to do with the ***beginnings.*** The word ***Genesis*** in the Hebrew language is *Bereshit* meaning *"in a beginning"*. The *beginnings of anything are FOUNDATIONAL* because they set the style, tone, mood, and values that will inform and shape the remainder of the project. **The *first 77 words of Genesis do this for me!***

The **fact** that the written Hebrew scriptures have been held and protected, copied and shared, for well over 2500 years of war, conflict, destruction, and massive cultural change is a testimony to their value in the *common human experience*. **Their authentic ongoing value to humanity** is grounded in roots that even precede their written form by give or take 1000 years. They have been shared orally, written down, and preserved because they continue to inform, inspire, and guide those who would learn from the Holy Divine Spirit Presence they embody, and to which they bear witness.

Moving *ever forward*!

 ~*PART ONE*~

LIFE COACH COMPASS QUESTIONS

Consider these questions as a COMPASS of PERCEPTION as you read.
[Right and wrong or correct and incorrect categories of judgment do not apply]

1] What does this story tell you about **the characteristics of a]** who God is; **b]** what God is like; **and c]** what God is concerned about? Every time you read a sentence or a story ask yourself questions like: **Who is God** here? What **is one characteristic** of God here? What **might God's intent or hope be** here?

2] What does this story tell you about **a]** the **nature of** and **b]** the **characteristics of *who we are as human beings***? As you read the story, stop and ask yourself **to**

identify 3 characteristics {adjectives} this story suggests that **we humans are like** as indicated by the information in or implications of the story. Then, extend the search to consider **what humanity as a whole is like**?

3] What does this story tell you about **a]** the **nature and characteristics of human relationships** with God, **b] human relationships with ourselves as unique individuals**, or **our personalities**, and **c]** humans as **people in relationship with other people?**

4] As you read ask yourself these questions: **What one characteristic does *this story* tell us about *our relationship* with God?** What **stands out in this story** about **what we human beings are like? What two characteristics or adjectives** you would choose in **describing the relationship between the individual characters in this story?**

This COMPASS ✣ will guide you as a reader while helping you to discern subjective personal meaning from the characters, their actions, and the choices the story tellers have assigned to them. As you identify and follow your personal responses like my dog following a trail of treats when playing "find it", you may discover new awareness and guidance through many subjective situations, meanings, or implications. Even when the story describes a characteristic or behavior you want to avoid or reject, you will have more from which to make your own choices.

There is a saying among wood working craftspeople that states:
"Time follows Quality". Lower quality moves fast while higher quality takes more time.

COLLECTING KEYS

KEYS open locks. Keys enable one to pass through previously locked and blocked spaces of understanding. My hope is for you to look for your own personal KEYS within what I offer. You are reading about keys that unlocked discoveries which might hopefully be of assistance to you *in your* discoveries. Who knows about that!? **Only YOU**.

KEY # 1: Looking behind and beyond the *facts*.

Somewhere along the road of life I realized that **every story** held potential meaning beyond its *factual information*. I learned to look within the interplay of the characters involved in the telling of the tale for clues on meaning beyond their situation. Every story has built-in invisible arrows pointing this way and that in the direction of meaning and/or *truth* that is beyond either the historical facts **or** the dialogue of the characters in the story. A **KEY ATTITUDE** is to become an investigator of meaning. **Look beyond the obvious and ask what life meaning might be discovered.**

If I were to ask only the simple logical question of the text, *"Is this story factual or true?"*, I automatically reduce it to being largely irrelevant regarding important aspects of life in the here and now. It can then *offer little* other than to provide some level of comfort or assurance. At one point I realized it doesn't matter so much if a story from the ancient past is factual or historically *true-accurate*. **What matters is to discover meaning in a** story that may inform or transform my understanding or relationship with, "*What is true or accurate for me right now?!*" That is the question I'm inviting **you to ask** for yourself!

I seek the answer to this very important and far reaching question: *"What about this story has anything to do with me, or my fellow humans, or in the case of the Bible, God?"* **My response is to apply my imagination in asking questions of meaning that go beyond the facts or historical information** of the story. I open my mind and my imagination, and **let the story tell me what it wants me to know** about life, truth, God, or myself. THAT is the question I ask: *"Hey story,* **What do you want to tell me about God, my neighbor, myself and my life?"**

KEY # 2: The gift of a Paradox

The dictionary states that a paradox is "*a seemingly absurd or self-contradictory statement or proposition that when investigated or explained may prove to be well founded or true.*" The paradoxical guidance *I have personally learned to follow* when reading the Bible [and almost all other scriptures] is: **1)** FIRST: to *accept any and all information and dialogue in the Biblical text as it reads* **regardless** of its inconsistent, contradictory, unscientific, or illogical, nature. **Accept it and begin with it as it is. 2)** SECOND: To complete the paradox, do not continue with the expectation or need for any information regarding factual historical events, records, or the exact dialogue between any characters to have any basis in what actually may, could have, or did happen in the past, **and** would be what **you would have witnessed** had you been present at that circumstance filming with your iPhone.

To do that would be to set yourself up to read the text as an analytical historian whose quest will not reveal the essence, character and nature of God, God's dynamic *Way*, or values beyond superficial rules. **An example for you is this:** When you encounter a RULE like in Genesis chapter 2, *"But of the tree of knowledge, good and evil, you shall not eat,…"* I encourage you to ask yourself this kind of question: *"What about that rule is important? What's the big deal? What might happen to me if I broke the rule? Doomed to die? What does that mean? What kind of death might it be? What kind of tree is one with a name like that? I have never even heard of that kind of tree, and what kind of fruit might it grow/produce?"* [I am writing a second book to address Genesis chapter 2]

To limit the text to its observable literal meaning will not reveal the complex nature of what it means to be a human being created by and loved by an amazing Creator Spirit who is taking a life-long trip with you as you travel the days of your life here on *Planet Earth University*.

Why did I come to this conclusion? Because we live in a time when the words of Joseph Campbell have described our cultural circumstances when he talked about *the guiding mythical and mystical traditions from our past that gave rise to religions and cultural values in the past influencing and guiding our predecessors have* **become mostly disconnected** *from our modern stories and understanding of the world in which we live. When I read in his book "Pathways to Bliss" these words: "It is largely from the psychological standpoint that one can reinterpret, re-experience, and reuse the great mythical traditions.",* I thought to myself, *Dude! That's what I realized back in 1974, and I didn't know anyone else had a similar awareness!* I didn't know it back then, but to be a Life Coach and interpreting these ancient stories into relatable psychological reality is what I was born to do.

I've been doing that with the scriptures from very early in my ministry.

Even as the ancient stories of Genesis are scientifically, historically, and factually disconnected from our 21st century understanding of the world and the physical circumstances in which we live, *our humanity's fundamental emotional and relational challenges, as well as our common psychological developmental needs are very similar to those ancient people.* **It's our being a member of the HUMAN RACE that we have in common, and that's the CORE of the Biblical Story from front to back.** *Look for the Human relationships through which God establishes experiences as they **lead** us to grow on multiple levels.*

> **Author's Note:** *My hope is that you will discover an important, honest and true meaning for **your life** in every story, every character, every relationship, every description, every dialogue, and every action ascribed to God, and all the crazy unique characters that fill the book of Genesis. The issue is **to discover for yourself** meaning that resides in the stories through the action between characters, or the responses of those characters. It is inappropriate to ask you to conform to another persons or institution's focus on what is valuable. Certainly, others who have experienced the story may provide understanding or meaning that for them is valuable, but only you can decide if their value is your value. While no one can be the first person to encounter these stories, and we all learn from others, each of us is assigned to decide what to adopt and what to leave out as we travel along the way.*

KEY #3: Use your imagination to go into the distant past

Close your eyes.... *[OOOPs, Open your eyes. Hard to read with your eyes closed!]* **Engage your imagination:** Go back in time say, 3000 years before today. You're in a small village in the hill country on the Eastern end of the

Mediterranean Sea. Imagine yourself gathered around the communal fire with several relatives. You have been reared among a small number of families [mostly related to you] who have crops and herds of animals. You live in a large tribe with a name taken from one of the son's of the great patriarch Jacob/Israel. Sometimes in the evening you hear stories from the elders about how a great God has formed all that you can see or imagine, and who watches over you and your family as a loving parent might do. You don't question theses stories, you just listen and learn. Unknowingly you are the recipient of an ORAL tradition informing you of meaning, value, and a sense of belonging to something that has been forming and informing your family and many families before you for a thousand years. It is important to remember these origins as you are encouraged to explore meaning through asking **"why" questions**.

Consider asking *"I wonder why?"* questions:
1) Why did the original story tellers put the story together **exactly the way they did**? 2) Why did they include these characters? 3) Why did the characters interact with God, or one another, or within their own thoughts and feelings **in the way they did** in the story? 4) What **might have been their intention** in including the dialogue that you find in the story? These are questions that may come to mind when you, the reader are freed from the perception that you are reading an accurate report of an historical event.

Once a person accepts that the story tellers are not reporting an historical event witnessed exactly like it happened, and that no one was around as a witness either confirming or denying the factual truth of the story as it is presented, **THEN, we are FREE** to consider the possible **INTENTION of the story teller,** especially as the story has been passed down from generation to generation. Now the listener/reader can benefit in asking: *"What were they thinking or intending when they included the unique packages of information, or sequence of events, or expressions of the thoughts or emotions of God, or a human character in the story?"* I **wonder why** they chose to include "this or that"? I **wonder why** they included this story and left out another? The questions give you a way to discover meaning for your life. **That is a foundational issue in all of your interaction with the scripture.**

An Example:
Regarding the content of the first two chapters in Genesis: Why did they include two different stories about creation rather than just one? I wonder what meanings or messages they intended or hoped the reader might discover? Were they thinking about who might hear these stories many years later? Did they need the stories to give credibility to something going on between competing factions in their day and time? Why did they choose to remember the behavior or dialogue given to individual characters? Did they have differing views of the character and nature of God? Did they hope the readers would have discussions among themselves over the variety of perspectives and in doing so learn things in that process they might never have considered? Absolutely!

The **"WONDER" questions** are intended to get your **mind and heart engaged in the Bible story.** THIS is one way we ALLOW the Bible to come alive in our being. We are encouraged to ASK QUESTIONS FOR WHICH THERE may be NO CORRECT CLEAN CLEAR PURE ANSWER! **Your responses to the questions are the important focus. What we ask will tell us more about ourselves and our spiritual journey than it will about the text!**

Sometimes leaders of religious groups both large and small will themselves invite-threaten-require you TO

AVOID ASKING QUESTIONS. There may be hidden agendas. They may be desiring to be in control; to claim power, and to keep a sense of order. They may want **to be the authority who finally decides** what something means. They may want **to limit the possibilities of interpretation and meaning** to something they can more easily manage. It is sometimes chaotic to have multiple perspectives on the same thing. The cohesion of the group is threatened when there are disagreements on meaning or intent. Especially in those settings where leaders value harmonious agreement more than discussion centered learning.

Religious ORGANIZATIONS prosper when everyone in the group thinks SIMILARLY or ALIKE. I've witnessed strong leaders limit their congregation's access to the Bible by authorizing only one translation of the Bible as acceptable because having a variety of translations reflects the amazing diversity of translating from the Hebrew, *[or in the case of the New Testament Greek scriptures],* and using only ONE agreed upon set of translated words and thoughts from which to discern and apply meaning. That cleans things up. To limit the interpretation of the Hebrew text *{remember all of the Old Testament was originally written in Hebrew}* **to only one possible meaning in ENGLISH** is sometimes impossible and mostly very challenging. Even though it may appear desirable to those who have a strong need to know the EXACT TRUE MEANING of something. The reality is that **in the original Hebrew writings** there appear well over a hundred Hebrew words that have no definitive context or a second appearance in the text to help translators assign a definitive meaning for the word.

While you may be willing to hand your authority over to someone or something else because it seems frightening or overwhelming to accept personal responsibility for what the text means in your life, the

bottom line is that* FINALLY,** *you will always be the final authority* regarding how to relate to the text and how you apply its meaning and value to your life.*** Emotional pressure from your clan or group of influence may be strong, but **finally YOU are the one authority for your life.** If you give it to another, it is you who have given it away. See your life as a gift from God's loving grace filled **TRUST** in your ability to claim **the power** to make decisions that serve you best at that time.

🗝 KEY #4: *How we measure time*

Please consider the idea of TIME with me for a moment. *Time itself is a construction of our being a human being responding to our human experience on Earth.* We need a way to discern and measure movement in our world. There is movement from one place to another and one behavior to another. Both of these lift up our awareness that they require TIME.

Our growth and development is a process involving time. Dr Mario Martinez points out in his book *"The MindBody Code"* that *"It is essential to recognize **time** as an invention we devised to measure our movement through space."*.[The Mind Body Code page 94] He pointed out how our primal ancestors wondered around in history living in the immediate present and had no concept of past or future. However, once they begin to make tools used in a certain situation to accomplish an important task, **they became aware that later in time** they might need the same tool for the same task therefore, saving the tools for the future need. He feels this meant they had formed the connections in their brains to conceptualize *time*.

It is important for us to be aware that we read the Hebrew scriptures from our current cultural awareness. We experience both a vast resource of historical information available to us from our past, as well as multiple 24 hour news outlets sharing current information about events around the globe *as it is happening in the present.* This environment is an extreme CONTRAST to those ancient cultures. As we attempt to to realize how we are creatures who have constructed time it is very important to remember that TIME does not control us. It is a tool. We manage our relationship to time.

We must realize that **determining the factual dates** of any event or situation in the Hebrew scriptures is NOT an exact science. **It is almost ALWAYS an educated guess.** The Hebrews did not keep historical records as we modern western scientific analytical people do. What might at first appear to be the "factual history" included in the Biblical text is much more of a **THEOLOGICAL DOCUMENT** than it is a **reliable factual historical record.** They told **"His-story"** with a theological agenda focused on revealing God's WAY, God's character, or intent in relationship to God's people and their lives. A term coined by German Biblical scholars in the late 19th century calls the Bible's seemingly historical narratives by the name **"Salvation History"**, **because it is "History written to reveal the personal redemptive activity of God within human history."** [Johann Christian Konrad von Hofmann - *Wikipedia*] It's like a class of learners asking a great teacher the question, *"What is God like?"* with Her response being: *"You want to know **what God is like**, let me tell you a story…". "You want to know **why we are here**, let me tell you a story…". "You want to know **why there is evil in the world**, let me tell you a story…"*

Biblical scholars, archeologists, anthropologists, and historical researchers attempting to discover **solid factual, provable information** that could confirm records and dates within the scriptures realized *through their experience* that the best information was found in records of the larger civilizations that interacted with the

Hebrews. That would provide a *second witness* confirmation of something that did or did not happen between their forces of war and/or commerce confirming an historical report in the Bible's narrative. The Hebrews with their roots in the ancient past had no interest in recording their factual history until the time of the historian Josephus who was born in in the year 37 of the Common Era.

Author's Note:
How the modern world keeps time.
*The term "**B**efore the **C**ommon **E**ra" —**BCE** implies a modern reference on time keeping which honors the various cultural time measuring systems by the world's religions and cultures - Chinese, Jewish, Hindu, Muslim. It establishes a **Common** counting system on behalf of commerce and world wide communication. The "**C**ommon **E**ra" {**CE**} begins with the influence of the Christian calendar and the selected starting date being the birth or conception (?) of Jesus Christ which is established as year "**0**". Commercial interests and governments across the world have generally agreed to follow this system. While **BCE** begins with "0"and gets larger **as <u>one goes further back</u>** in time. **CE** [the **C**ommon **E**ra] begins with "0"and gets larger **as <u>one moves forward</u>** in the direction of the present.*

***ONE MORE THING** that can lead to confusion. For over 1000 years Christians who dominated life in Western culture adopted the **Latin term 'AD'** which is short for **'Anno Domini'** [in English meaning: 'the year of our Lord'] **to be associated with counting all the years following the birth of Christ**, and that (**BC**) **B**efore **C**hrist would be added to all of the years **preceding** the birth of Christ.*

KEY #5: Setting the stage

MOST people experience emotional STRESS when they encounter rapid changes. It seems that our current culture is filled with rapid changes every day. Earlier in KEY 3, I asked you to go back in time to a time when change was very slow indeed. Here is the Hebrew's story from that *slow to change* time in their history. Larger civilizations with overpowering force outside the boundaries of Israel so disrupted their culture, their religion, and their way of life that the stress they experienced over a long period of years led to an eventual change in how they understood themselves, their culture, and way of life.

They had been taught for hundreds of years that **if they followed God's rules and did what they were taught** *God wanted God's chosen people* **to do, that God would protect them from harm**.

Like most of us, the **disconnect came** in the reality of their **actual EXPERIENCE.** From documents found in the records of the ancient nation of *Assyria*, a much larger nation to the North and East of Israel, and subsequently in the *Babylonian* records after they defeated the Assyrians, the *Hebrews in the land of Israel/ Judah* were involved in a serious internal spiritual/cultural/religious **crisis** caused by these large nations who came into their land, defeated their armies, laid siege to their cities, and took them captive. God did NOT MEET their expectations of being protected from their enemies.

These *factually* true events- *as much as anyone can discern truth from ancient history* - would lead to the faith stories of the **oral tradition** becoming changed into a **written stories** that would outlive the guardians and story tellers who may be killed in future unknown events.

In 722 BCE the Assyrians defeated and carried off the ***10 Northern tribes*** of the nation of Israel. Assyrians separated them from their fellow countrymen, then scattered and integrated them into the Assyrian culture spread throughout their vast empire. As far as historians can determine the unique Hebrew cultural identity and history of those 10 northern tribes were lost to both history and to the future for all time. This is why they are sometimes referred to as the *10 Lost Tribes of Israel*.

*A **Quick history** many people do not know leading up to this situation!*
After the death of King Solomon, his two sons competed for the throne. There was a power struggle. Each son proclaimed his vision of how he wanted to lead and his values. The people were given the right to choose between the two sons. Of the twelve tribes of Israel, 10 of the tribes who had been assigned land in the northern part of the country chose one son as king, while the priestly tribe of the Levites, and the tribe of Judah chose the other son as king. The Northern group was called **Israel,** and the Southern group was called **Judah**. **Israel** was more nationalistic with great pride, and when the larger nation of Assyria invaded, The Israelites fought… **and lost**. The tribe of Judah negotiated and was allowed to maintain their unique identity and pay tribute to Assyria. After 722 BCE only 2 tribes remained; the **tribe of Judah of the Southern Kingdom**, and the **priestly tribe of Levites**.

In 626 BCE Babylonia defeated the Assyrians, and by 597 BCE had laid siege to Jerusalem [in Judah] after defeating Egyptian Pharaoh Necho with whom Judah had a defensive protection agreement. In 586 they finally overwhelmed Jerusalem and carried all the cultural leaders and important Jewish families off to Babylonia. But **unlike the Assyrians before them, they allowed the Jews to live in compounds where they were able to maintain their unique Jewish cultural identity.**

The point to all of this: The Hebrews/Jews began to reflect on the *new world order and* **realized they lived in a changing, challenging, and sometimes threatening situation.** *[Did you notice how many years the*

Babylonians laid siege to Jerusalem? Subtract 586 from 597 = they held out eleven years!] The Jews were a smart people, but **like all people they resisted change.** While Babylonia allowed them to keep, maintain, and practice their religious traditions, **it also compelled them to realize that** *as the keepers of the sacred stories and those charged to be leaders of their faith tradition,* they needed to begin the process of *transferring the spoken stories of the oral tradition into a more stable written form.*

Life Coach Notes: *Converting their oral stories to writing was a challenging and radical idea for a people whose oral tradition had served them for over 700 years! — Stop and compare: How long has the United States of America has been in existence?* **We all have difficulty with change** *in some form or another.*

Do you recognize normal human behavior in this situation? You know about being forced by large unwanted circumstances beyond your control **calling you to make uncomfortable changes in your life***, do you not? Consider the issues in the early 21st century, such as facing rapid global climate change and a global pandemic of COVID. So much must be changed in our complex world requiring people to acknowledge the problem and work together to make a difference before life becomes increasingly difficult. Things were challenging for those ancient people, and we have a similar struggle in our world, just a different set of contents.*

By 539 BCE the Persians under King Cyrus had defeated Babylon and in 538 BCE he allowed the captive Jews to return home to Judah. What followed was a time of renewed commitment to God's law and tradition that began under the reign of King Josiah of Judah between 640 and 609 BCE. Scholars and historians believe this was the critical period when the Jews became active in the slow and sketchy process of transferring the stories of the oral tradition into writing . This process would continue over the next 500 years. **By the first century**

BCE the individual scrolls were assembled into what we today might begin to recognize as the *Hebrew Bible*.

Consider the Written Hebrew Language for a moment:
The Hebrew language did not originally have what modern language considers an essential element: **vowels**. I tell you that so you can appreciate the efforts Jewish scribes had to expend as they converted these spoken stories into a written language. Then later scribes in the early period of the Common Era [CE], adapted all of the written stories and text to include vowels by making certain marks around the Hebrew letters indicating which vowels should be added to the consonants to shape words. **Translating from these sources is NOT an exact science for even the best scholars.** We readers of English translations need to consider and appreciate the collective effort and insight which has gone into what we read today. It began 2500 years ago!

AUTHOR'S NOTE:
The very fact that we have **something in hand to read** as the printed Hebrew and Greek testaments, is a downright unrealistic and unexplainable miracle. The Holy Divine Creator Spirit and Origin of All that Is, IS somehow living in these words, and in the Spirit they embody through mystery, tradition, and physical human history. Perhaps it is still with us because of ALL its innate messiness, complexity, confusion, reluctance, fear, love, and insight. It is SO HUMAN! When we hold it in our hands I believe we hold a miracle even though it is so difficult to understand and integrate into our lives. Consider this: How many Mesopotamian stories of creation, or Greek history myths, or Egyptian God stories are in common print at your local Walmart?

THE INFLUENCE OF ORAL TRADITION

One evening after dinner when the dishes were washed and put away my mother called me to sit beside her on the couch in our den. I remember being in the 4th grade, and at the time when she asked I didn't know what to think. This was an unusual event. She motioned me to sit beside her on the couch, and opened a book I had never seen before. She began to read a story about a family much like ours [two parents and two children] who had gathered together to read the Bible. It was like I was listening to their family read and talk about the Bible while at the same time I learned Bible stories. We heard stories about King David and his early exploits with the giant Goliath, and of his friendship with Jonathan the son of King Saul. In my emotional memory, this was the only time my mother ever read to me. It had a powerful impact on my spiritual growth that I **only** recognized as an adult in my thirties while reflecting on why I loved the stories of the Hebrew Bible so much. *"Oh, I thought, it was that time in the 4th grade when mom read those stories to me from that series of books…"*. *[When my mom died some years ago I made certain I gathered and saved the 5 book series when we cleaned out her house.]*

My mother was a woman of duty, honor, and order. As a responsible Christian mother, she must have felt mildly obligated to read Bible stories to me. I can only believe that God's Spirit led her to gather me up that evening when my insurance salesman father was on an insurance call, and begin reading to me. *[We had no television.]* I can almost hear her voice now. It wasn't dramatic, but she was a good reader, and her voice felt comforting and close. It's like both Spirit and intimacy were all packaged together in that one experience.

Use your imagination again, and think of yourself going back in a time long before the modern era, when scrolls are the books in your Jewish community and no one family will have access to them. You're seated with your family at home for Friday evening worship, or Shabbat. It's family story time and your parents share the responsibilities for the story each night. Because this is my imaginal story, I decided it was your mother's turn to tell you tonight's story. She had learned it from her parents when she was your age, and it was told over and over again so that by the time she was an adult it was part of her everyday memory. And because the stories were integrated into her daily life, they informed her relationship to her family, her daily activities and how she viewed her world. It was **a *way* of life** far more important than just following a list of rules she was obliged to follow.

As I reflect on the Hebrew oral tradition, I believe the act of parents sharing their faith stories with their children had a powerful impact on both the individuals, the family base, and the religious foundations of the community. It gave the children a sense of belonging and personal inclusion as important participants in the community as well as being part of God's family and God's purposes. I also believe it nurtured intimacy between parent and child.

The power of these stories gave each young Jewish child a sense of collective identity that held them together as a culture over a long period of time. While the larger surrounding cultures of Egypt, Assyria, Babylonia, and Persia have in many respects come and gone over time, the Jewish tradition and its unique identity has remained very present even under constant scrutiny, social pressure, and persecution. **Consider that historically and factually,** *Israel is the only nation in the history of* *the world that was driven out of history in 70 CE by Roman forces, and then popped back into history in 1948 CE following WW II.* After being continually persecuted and oppressed by other peoples and cultures for over 1800 years, **their story held them as a people with a clear identity, and brought them back into modern history where they remain a powerful force.**

As a teacher and life coach I am clear that when a story is shared in an intimate way from parent to child it becomes a living story. With each telling, the story may have shifted or changed in ways that keep it culturally and personally relevant, emotionally fresh, and alive to the individuals who heard it. The human voice is so powerful at conveying subtleties of value, feeling, and inferred meaning beyond just the content of the story's words. Stories stand a good chance of coming alive in the hearts and minds of the listeners when someone they love is telling it. That's to say nothing of the importance of the bonding relationship between a father or mother telling stories to their children. As children listen, they soak up the intimacy of their parents' voices. The lived example the parents offer to the children by caring enough, and valuing the stories enough to gather their children together to listen even when the children are naturally resistant is a powerful witness. Stories of an oral tradition are a reflection of a Living Spiritual Presence that compels both the story teller and the listener, while at the same time forming a Spiritual bond bringing 'Spirit' to life in the heart of the next generation.

Cynics steeped in values of objective unchangeable historical truth and analytical cross referenced facts may see this variable-story-telling characteristic less as a flexible gift reflecting the subjective ever-present changes in life's circumstances, and more as a possible opportunity for subjective manipulation, inconsistency, and factual undependability. They may be unwilling to risk placing their trust or confidence in the authenticity of the text itself. That's everyone's choice. Each person must decide for themselves about the issue of authenticity, truth, and meaning as we filter any story through our own sense of what is true.

A CONTRADICTION in the Written Word. Since Genesis and all the Hebrew Scriptures in general became written down, they have over time been elevated to the status of an unchangeable *icon* containing *objective factual truth*. As such, the dynamic honesty of our sometimes messy, human faith-life stories often go unrecognized and even condemned in the effort to **objectify or fix the text. Fixed texts and corresponding fixed interpretations do not lend themselves to the adjustable needs of a living dynamic evolution within a human life or society.** This has historically led to powerful disagreements, conflicts, persecutions, political power struggles, and war when differing opinions are naturally encountered.

Institutional religion itself has a natural built-in proclivity to develop and adopt practices characterized by *unquestionable fixed dogma and consistent doctrine*. That's sometimes helpful for the left brain dominated brain wiring of some individuals, but in my experience it will at the same time lend itself to being used to judge, vilify and/or persecute those with differing opinions who call into question religion's accepted and decreed truth. Bureaucrats in any institution will be threatened by individuals who offer differing viewpoints. *[For example, the real story of Christ's persecution and death.]* As the study of church history will dramatize, institutional leaders/authorities are prone to promote the cleansing of the faith to maintain their personal ***illusions of purity*** even if it means killing those who hold contrasting opinions. *"We cannot allow the purity of our faith to be *threatened by these sinful ideas!"* This is a value system shared among many religious traditions.

> ***Author's Note:*** *It seems that many people have been unable or unwilling to reflect upon the truth/experience of their own lives leading them to realize that **the idea of PURITY is a dreamy ILLUSION** that is unsuited to measure belief, faith or to keep as a realistic goal within life's value systems. Purity is a standard best applied to drinking water, and not to faith or the living of an authentic integrated life with all of it's real messiness! The possibility of Grace abounds!*

A shining example of the abusive nature of the focus on doctrinal purity:

When considering the earliest scientific awareness of our solar system by Copernicus and Galileo we can see a perfect storm of conflict between the revelations of science and the established authority of an institutional religious story-tradition that interprets and accepts the stories of the Bible as the factual, historical, bearer of scientific truth to be defended and enforced without modification. As Copernicus published in 1543 CE, and Galileo supported the research showing that the Earth was NOT the center of the universe and that all the planets revolved around the Sun, *[A heliocentric solar system]* It became a radical challenge to the theological world view of the Roman Church -*the dominant form of Christianity at the time*- and was totally rejected. In 1633 CE Galileo was condemned and threatened with torture by the authority of the church until he recanted his belief and support of Copernicus. He died in 1642 CE under house arrest at the age 77 because of his views. Then 350 years later, on October 31,1992 CE, *[All Hallows Eve, the day preceding All Saints Day when in the Christian tradition remembers and celebrates all the dead saints of the church.]* - the Roman Catholic Church under Pope John Paul II **finally admitted** that Galileo was correct in adopting Copernicus' observations that the Earth rotates around the Sun and that the Earth is therefore **not** the center of the universe as accepted and defended by church doctrine. I believe that to be a belated 'tip of the hat' to the *authentic saints* who were persecuted by the church because they would not recant the scientific truth of their convictions.

> *"Every time you find in our books a tale the reality of which seems impossible, a story which is repugnant both to reason and common sense, then be sure that tale contains a profound allegory veiling a deeply mysterious truth… and the greater the absurdity of the letter the deeper the wisdom of the spirit."*
>
> — Rabbi Moses ben Maimon
> [1135- 1204 CE]

PRAYER TIME:

Lord of love and creative movement, you who are the origin of change and expansion; we turn to you on this day as those who have made the turn into what might be possible with new perception and new knowledge. Yes, we confess that process to be both fearful and tiring, but for the moment we've decided to turn our faces into the wind of the future if only because where we are today is really where we've been for too long. We seek your companionship. We need your wisdom. We reach out knowing you care. Open our seeing to recognize what will lead us into new possibility. Beckon us toward what we might become in order to form another Source for your Light shining like the sun into the darkness of fear and separation. We trust your love. We hope in the future. We're glad your our friend. Amen.

SETTING UP THE FIRST CREATION STORY

The first 77 words comprising the first 5 verses of Genesis chapter 1 will both set a pattern and establish a process for discerning meaning from the text as you might choose to read further.

This first Creation story in Genesis reads like something that might have been discovered in a pile of rubble from some archeological site containing directions for the general steps to building a large house. The steps described in the 6 day sequence [beyond the first 77 words] hold a series of intentions and actions following logically one after another. There is **first the lightbulb of an idea or vision** of the project *[to create 'heaven and earth']* that is followed by **showing up on the scene** *[God's presence 'hovers']*, then **site preparation for the foundation** *[built on dry land separated from the water in rivers and lakes]*, the **construction of a dome** *[building a frame]* **with a top** *[roof holding out the water from above]* and **an expansive vault-firmament dome** holding and separating water that's above from the water which is below *[keeping the structure safe and dry]*. Then within the vault of the structure **the creator fills the firmament** *[like putting furniture, plants and decor in the house]* with all that is needed to make earth into a beautiful garden-like-home in the spirit of a super sized terrarium. I can't help but believe those ancient story tellers had a similar idea in their intuition about the **way** they viewed their world. [Explanation: the **way** is a code phrase that sums up in a word the attitude, the process, the life style, and the value system of the dynamic **way of faith** as lived in life.]

I get it! The other day I was outside working in the yard and looked into the sky while forgetting all I know about earth, atmosphere, the solar system and the larger cosmos in general. My imagination could easily have developed a wonderful story about the round dome of blue sky above that covered the flat surface of the round earth within the perspective of my view. As a person who has spent many hours in out-of-doors settings watching the world around me being filled with wildlife and so many of the items listed in the Bible story's menu of creation, I could feel the possibility, the safety, the beauty, and the wonder that exists all around me. I can sense the *thin places of spirit* on earth even now from time to time. I suspect those early story tellers who lived so close to nature had a great sense of this story's origin source and its practical meaning for their lives.

In my life these stories have provided a framework of understanding which has guided my perceptions, values, and attitudes. They reveal patterns that will for all time be a core guiding instinct of our human experience if we can see into the deeper meaning they offer. It doesn't matter if the focus of our attention is creating houses, buildings, businesses, a marriage, rearing children, or forming a lump of clay into a useful shape as in the hands of a potter, **there is an underlying common thread of attitude, experience, challenge and reward that mixes in and through our lives.** The *intuition and inspiration* of some deep inner consciousness *[I choose to call the Spirit of God]* the Hebrews perceived, constructed into language, shared, and finally wrote into history was because somehow their intuition sensed and recognized at some deep level a *common human story* which is at the core of the *God and Human* experience. We benefit as we learn from it. We stumble when we don't.

When we take the time to explore the **"Beginnings"** we find the opportunity to better understand the fundamental stories of the root experiences extending back to the emergence of our human theological recognition of the Mysterious Spirit Presence beyond comprehension. LET'S DIVE IN!

PART TWO

The First 77 Words of Genesis:

Inspired by the Biblical Translation **"The Five Books of Moses,"**
by Professor Robert Alter

He is the Winner of PEN Center Literary Award for Translation and the
Koret Jewish Book Award and Robert Kirsch Award from Lifetime Achievement from
the Los Angeles Times. He is Emeritus Class of 1937 Professor of Hebrew and
Comparative Literature at the University of California, Berkeley

Genesis 1:1a "When God began to create heaven and earth,..."

When I first came across Robert Alter's new translation of the Hebrew scriptures, my internal spirit lit up because of my lifelong love affair with Genesis. I ordered all three volumes and immediately opened his translation of the first five books of the Bible generally known as the Pentateuch or Torah, or, as his Jewish tradition calls them, *the Five Books of Moses*. **I soon discovered in Genesis 1, words and phrases placed in a manner that seemed almost as if I had never seen them before.** I was captured. As my eyes read the first 8 words in this order, I found myself experiencing a surprising light of clarity shining new insight on a story I had seen hundreds of times. He translates Genesis 1: ***"When God BEGAN to create heaven and earth,…"***

All my life I had only read the words *"In the beginning God…"* followed by the familiar. Most popular translations of the Bible begin with some form of: *"In the beginning God…"*. Professor Alter's translation begins ***"When God began…"***.

Three important and unique characteristics of his translation:

First: Because he is the **lone translator** of this work, and not part of a **translation committee** like most every other English translation of the scriptures *[Including the King James version]*. He is free to share his best understanding of the actual Hebrew words without regard to tradition, church doctrine, what people might expect of a translation, **or** for published literature asking the commercial question: "What do the people paying for this translation want?" They need to sell a lot of books! Book sellers know, *"don't rock the cultural boat if you want to sell a lot of books!"* Commercial interests aim for the demographic that will sell the most, and make it fit what is expected.

Second: The actual Hebrew doesn't exactly read, *"In the beginning God"*… Scholars who read Hebrew have known this for many years. The phrase, *"In the beginning God"* is just one interpretation, and it is largely based on the institutional values and needs of the early Christian movement. That interpretation had always **led me to believe there was nothing created before God started the creation process**. The picture in my mind had been **that everything was nothing more than a vast emptiness** from which God began to create from *nothing* as in a vacuum. What you want to believe is your choice, but *"In the Beginning God…"* is NOT the best way to read this Hebrew story. It is certainly not the **only** correct and exact interpretation. Read on!

Third: The phrase **"When God began to create heaven and earth,…" describes the scope of God's intent.** For the storytellers, the idea of *heaven and earth* **indicates all they knew or could know** regarding the world in which they lived. *Heaven and earth* were spacial entities. Heaven was **the sky** and all they could see with their eyes from where they were looking up and out. **Heaven** had **no reference or awareness** to some location for life after death. It was the sky and everything that was *up there or out there.* The **earth** was the land and water and all they could see with regards to the *solid stuff* upon which they stood. Earth was not a spherical planet moving through space turning one revolution each day while it made its 365 day trip around the sun. The *scope of this story* is limited to what *they understood* as God's intended goal to create *heaven and earth* for all of humanity. This was all that was observable and *experienceable* by humans at the time they created this story.

Here's the factual piece of history I was never taught: *"In the Beginning"* became the story of the traditional Christian church at a period when the earliest Christian movement was in formation around the 2nd Century of the Common Era. Christianity's factually documented history of adopting this phrase is this: Sometime in the second century CE, a man named Theophilus of Antioch wrote to another man, Autocylus, that **"God created all things from nothing by the word of God."** This was the notion called **creation *"ex nihilo"* *-creation from nothing- in Latin.*** By the third century that idea became what would become the Roman Catholic Church made into a "doctrine of truth." Creation *"ex nihilo"* became a fundamental tenet of main-line Christian theology. One is compelled to *"believe it, or be in trouble with the institution that controls your eternal destiny".* The process behind this is common: identify the factual truth, adopt it as a fixed reality, build your perception of the world on it, and defend it.

Anything that is new must establish a foothold in society if it is to be successful. I suspect the early church desperately needed to claim a strong sense of **authority** in which *their story about God was that "He" was the One, the first creator, and the final authority for the Church, the world, and beyond.* That claim evolved into the institutional church being generally accepted as God's manifested **body** on Earth. *[A sometimes dangerous thing!]* As with any earthly institution, there are serious contradictions with that level of power being associated with the institutional Church. It will almost always lead to destructive practices and heavy handed control in the quest to both gain and keep purity and power.

This early and most vulnerable Christian movement needed God to be the originator of all that has material form. When in the 4th century CE the Emperor Constantine made Christianity the state religion of Rome whose empire extended over vast stretches of land and diverse peoples with many religious practices, another new order and authority was needed. Within what we now know was their very limited view of the world and how it worked, their adoption of *creation ex nihilo* was only logical and even necessary.

In the 16th century, CE an emerging awareness from the European renaissance of an activity and discipline we call **science** began to lay a new **foundation of inquiry.** That movement led in the 20th century to the launch of the Hubble space telescope [1990 CE], when humanity would experience a revelation of previously unknown awareness to the wonders of creation being far beyond 13.8 billion earth years of age. The Hubble Space telescope expanded the concept of God's creation far beyond our earth, our solar system, or anything we might have previously imagined. Its photographs and data reveal the immeasurable scale of the material and energetic universe, and in doing so have given us a *new story of God's creation*. **As amazing as I believe the creation accounts in both Genesis chapter one and chapter two were to those who first told them,** *God is SO MUCH MORE AMAZING than anything any human could EVER have imagined.* I expect revelations to continue as our awareness becomes even more expanded.

To sum up: GOD IS BEGINNING TO CREATE HEAVEN AND EARTH.

Genesis 1:1, 2 "When God began to create heaven and earth and the earth then ..."

The new awareness that there was so much more meaning to the first phrase of Genesis chapter one than just being a mis-guided science-history report from an ancient culture was totally freeing to me. God is in the process of beginning to *create heaven and earth!* But HOW, and with WHAT? *There's going to be some creating going on so tell me more!*

Upon God's decision to begin creating heaven and earth, the undisputed translations read, **"and the earth then… ."** **WHAT?** This indicates clearly that **in this story**, the **earth already existed before God began doing anything!** That is actually part of the translation that even *the committee translations* agree on. There are differing descriptions of what *"the Earth then"* was like, but all the translations of the original Hebrew **establishes clearly the idea** that the Earth was in existence before God started messing around with it in the process of creating heaven and earth.

As I realized this, I suddenly felt as if I was reading something much more important than a pre history fable attempting to explain how things came about wayback in time. I was instead reading a statement of faith by an ancient and amazing people **revealing to me both their picture and understanding of the primary characteristic of God:** *God was and is, first and foremost, a CREATOR who took "the earth then", and transformed it into a "heaven and earth!!!"*

God's creative project intends a *transformative change* from the "earth then" God first encounters!

Genesis 2a. "When God began to create heaven and earth and the earth then was welter and waste…"

Be patient with me while I say this again: the "committee translations" begin with the same inaccurate traditional phrase, "In the beginning", however, they have no disagreement with Dr. Alter describing **the state or status of the earth then. The earth then was pretty much an empty, void, useless, and barren mess.** Professor Alter writes in his footnotes that one of the two Hebrew words he translates as *"welter* and *waste"* literally means *"emptiness"* or *"futility" in Hebrew.* When you look up the definition of *welter* in an English dictionary, it means *"a large number of items in no particular order, or being a confused mass."* So Alter's sense of the Hebrew is to indicate that **when God comes upon the *Earth* then it was something like a confused mass of waste.**

What a perfect image! *In my imagination,* I picture the Earth just hanging around in space like a useless disorganized pile of garbage which *God comes across in Her daily stroll through the heavenly cosmos.* Then, suddenly God has a creative *idea* like we might get when we're out wandering around enjoying the day and feeling creative! God thinks, to God's self, *"Wouldn't it be a great idea to* **create something special** *today!?"* Then, *"Wow, here's a floating pile of useless garbage totally void of value, and life, but full of possibility to become something beautiful and interesting!"* *"I think I'll start here!"* What are your thoughts about how it might have gone down?

This might be mildly comparable to a car collector driving through a rural part of Connecticut during a sunny Saturday morning excursion, while following his intuition down a rural dirt road, where he discovers an amazing automotive *barn-find* of classic cars from 50 to 100 years old sitting neglected with discarded trash piled all around. The *welter and waste* of those classic automobiles needs a *creator* to value them, claim a vision for them, take them under his creative wing, and transform them into something amazing. So, from God's perspective **the**

Earth then needed a Holy Creator to transform it into a magnificent *"heaven and earth!"* **That is what I believe the text indicates is God's vision, desire, and intent. How might it seem to you?**

What is a characteristic of God in this story so far? God shows up **one day** -*before there were days*- with a **vision** to make this mass of discarded welter and waste into a most beautiful heaven and earth! When one **grounds** this story in meaning, **God's vision is to be the One who takes welter and waste in *our personal lives* and doesn't just condemn it, or *walk away Renee,* leaving it to float uselessly in space, or be condemned to a cosmic garbage pile. God does much *more*!** That's what we can know at this point from **this creation story: It** is about creative ***beginnings and a God Spirit Force who creates from welter and waste***.

The story continues to develop one phrase at a time:

Genesis 1: 2 "When God began to create heaven and earth and the earth then was welter and waste and darkness over the deep..."

The situation is even more challenging than we first thought for creating *heaven and earth* from *welter and waste*! We discover we have a **DARK DEEP DISORGANIZED mass of waste needing transformation**! It's a "triple D" mess!

The situation is portrayed as one in which the creator can't even SEE what a big *friggin* mess it's in, IT'S TOO DARK! All we know for certain is that it is dark and deep, and like, **WET**. Have you ever been underwater in total darkness? I haven't, but I've seen deep sea photography which shows just how DARK it gets at several miles down where the darkness just *swallows up* the light from the submersible craft exploring far below. I've personally been the captain of a pontoon boat on a large lake in the absolute darkness of a new moon, with no shore lights for navigation reference points. I am responsible to my family for finding our way back to the dock without crashing into a sand bar or other invisible floating debris. Even the light from a 500 lumen spotlight is just swallowed by the darkness of the water.

"AND darkness over the deep..." sounds like an **accumulation** of challenging circumstances potentially blocking the manifested creation of a wonderful vision called *heaven and earth*, RIGHT?

Life Coach Notes: If your life is anything like mine, I suspect there has been a time or two you might have had a similar set of circumstances: 1) a confused mass of waste confronting you as you strive to bring into manifested existence a wonderful vision, then, 2) The confrontation of compounded and confounded difficulty in newly discovered working conditions.

Sometimes things go from bad to worse. The first home we owned was on a one acre lot in a rural area served by a septic system. One day the sewer line collapsed creating a *welter and waste* situation that demanded attention. I called the plumber and within a few hours he had it analyzed and repaired. While working, I was asking him about how things were going, and he looked up and said, *"My daddy once told me that the way life works is about the time you think you're going to finally make ends meet, something comes along and moves one of them."*

I suspect anyone reading this will recognize their experience of **moving ends** and **dark places**.

> Maybe the challenge is in the necessity to make choices that put an end to one part of your life in order to embrace new possibility for the future. **There are hundreds of challenging emotions, circumstances, situations, and experiences throughout our lives, and this story announces that they might possibly be an opportunity to create our yet to be realized new possibility within your personal vision of creating a *heaven and earth for your life and that of your family*.** This story about God [Elohim] offers me what I believe to be the TRUTH, (if you are hunting for that sort of thing). It dramatizes that within the VERY FIRST ACT OF CREATION God has already been there, done that, and faces the difficulty head on. **That is good to know anytime we are expending our own efforts to create something new. God's character is experienced in the realm of earth's challenges.**

Wait a minute! Could it be that **this story** we thought was from some irrelevant remote ancient scientifically clueless culture having no awareness about the proven factual science we know today revealing a super important story reflecting the **fundamental** sense of what it means to be **living an authentic HUMAN life as a creation of God**?! Well, maybe, YES! I believe so! **But *your opinion* is the only one that matters to you!**

SUDDENLY we begin to realize this is a story rehearsing OUR HUMAN story. They're talking about *the earth then* being a totally inhospitable place God has chosen to make into *heaven and earth*, but can S/He do it? Is it worth the effort? That's a question we must ask **when we have a vision** and come across a similar circumstance of opportunity and challenge.

Consider how we work and play. **Isn't this something like the challenges we CONSTRUCT in our society to provide our human experience an opportunity to expand? We make games** where there is *conflict, challenge, and struggle designed into the challenges* to accomplish the goals of the game. We create *difficult challenges* for entertainment on television. We have hours and hours of sports that are built around organized conflicts. We have carefully conceived the structure of rules and defined areas of play to act out our challenges. If they're too difficult we may even rise above a previous human level of expertise to meet the new challenge. If it is too easy we become bored and turn away. There is something fundamentally in us at the root of our humanity, that is an expression of this story about God being challenged to **take a big weltering waste in the dark and deep,** and do something amazing with it. *I believe that has been passed down through thousands of generations to the degree that each of us has some large or small residue of that DNA living inside.*

At one point several years ago my oldest son was a contestant on the CBS television show *Survivor*. I believe he experienced a number of significant challenges to expand his abilities on multiple levels. The *game masters* that do all the conceptualizing and development of the situations and events had created activities and situations to test the participants on multiple levels in both personal and group achievement. Behind all those experiences were issues of strategy, attitude, spirit, and adaptability that became progressively more significant as the games progressed. **Why would anyone want or choose to do that?? What is it in the human experience that compels us to engage in such activities?? Could it be that IN the experience of each moment of the game, the issues of LIFE ITSELF are the** *real focus being dramatized and rehearsed* **over and over again?** I believe so. Tell me where I'm wrong.

CONSIDER what God is doing in this story. Could it be like a divine *home fixer-upper* project soon to appear on a new series called, "*Divine Home and Garden Television"?* You might imagine God speaking: *"Ok, contestants, we have a disorganized mess that you are going to turn into a new home for the deserving [and in*

God's grace the not so deserving] family of humanity. And here is one more part of the challenge we haven't told you yet: You have do do it in the dark while working up to your waist in water." **Sometimes there is darkness over the deep!**

Life Coach Notes:
If you still believe this is an insignificant fairy tale of an ancient people, consider this: God initiated the birth and continuation of all things from a CREATIVE CORE of CONSCIOUSNESS **that is fundamental to God's very nature,** *and* which I believe has been encoded into every human genome from birth till death. It is fundamental to our human nature that **every person** will have **some level of desire and anxiety** within their own set of unique skill sets, interests, focus, intensity, and personal insecurities that **will in some form arise at the thought of being exactly WHO they were created to be regardless of societies expectations.** From that, we will be pushed and compelled to find a way through the "welter and waste" of our lives to **MANIFEST** that unique personal *I AM-NESS* of our identity in some tangible manner or expression. *There's no-aspect of the story that indicates it will be easy!* Easy is boring! We humans cannot endure boring for long!

This awareness is *so important,* I'm going to spend more time with it.

Multiple popular HGTV or Magnolia Network shows focus on the 'star(s)' of the show discovering for a client their potential home/house/structure that is in need of transformation. Through their skill, vision, talents, imagination, and the efforts of a well skilled and financed team they begin to reimagine the structure into an amazing new *home* for a family. What might initially seem like a positive story with a guaranteed outcome is anything but. When we watch the **first step,** they must demolish all that currently exists within the structure making room for the new transformation, and *we realize* *another reality*. Even the parts that might be salvageable or potentially useful must be taken down to make way for transformation. They just rip it, toss it, break it and carry it off to the dump. One would never believe the transformation when seen from the *stage of welter and waste.* **The dream of what it could be** as an amazing beauty with abundant amenities for happy living by an individual or family must *stay alive and guide the process* in both the show and our lives.

In our lives the *welter and waste* sometimes happens in a relationship long before it becomes obvious that *demolition is required*. Those are typically challenging circumstances where sustaining **the initial vision of possibility** for our lives is difficult and essential. I believe that even in the television shows there are multiple set backs. Some we observe and some we do not. In your life and mine there are occasions upon which our VISION of what may **become** on the other side of painful demolition is also essential because it is NOT a guaranteed perfect outcome!

"But wait, there's a very special secret ingredient in this story!"

Genesis 1:1-2
"When God began to create heaven and earth and the earth then was welter and waste and darkness over the deep and God's breath ..."

With utmost significance the story adds one more *and*...

Author's Note
Translator Alter points out that the Hebrews liked to add **"ands"** *one after another* **without commas** *to emphasize a kind of what I call a "gathering fullness" where one ingredient is stacked on another indicating a special* **synergy** *in the situation among the grouping.* In the 24 words we have now examined from this first chapter of Genesis, 5 of them have been the word *and*. **This last *and* adds a component of *hope* that I believe is present in *every* situation and in all things. It is the *agent* through which one can radically claim the awareness, attitude, vision, love, and fundamental *trust* enabling a person to claim the possibility to *create* within our own lives.** *Here you go people,* **the next component of assistance: *"...and God's breath ..."***

Life Coach Notes:
This word *breath* is the symbol of God's living presence. We will encounter this **breath** later in Genesis 2. Translator Alter footnotes this word as ***"breath-wind-spirit"*** (the Hebrew word is ***ruah***). This is a story about how **God is present** in the wind over every human situation or condition, and ready to help **create** new possibility, new meaning, new awareness, and to assemble new possibility for the Earth, and it's creatures from previously unforeseen and unexpected resources.

In the story thus far God has envisioned new possibility for what appears to be a VOID, EMPTY, USELESS, TRACKLESS WASTE. As it turns out, frequently God may creatively use our personal **welter-y-wastie** as the **raw material for creating a vision which might bring forth a great new BECOMING in our lives.** I find that to be kind of a *God thing* in my personal experience. I've come to adopt the practice of keeping my radar turned on and circling, *ready to detect that breath-presence* in my life.

> **Author's Note:**
> There are some Christians from both the past and in current times who will desire to limit God's creative love only to those who have followed their particular story's conditions and requirements for being included in God's family. Maybe it would be limited to those who have "been saved", or those who faithfully follow prescribed rules, or belong to a certain church/sect/religious affiliation, or religion. **That is *not in this story*.** *It is developed at a later time, but remember this story is the beginning of the beginnings: it is GENESIS. All else will follow.*

Here is the question we all encounter: Can you, **can we,** trust this hovering ruah-breath presence in our lives? That is the silent question being asked as an invisible thread running from Genesis 1 to Revelation 22. [The last book in the Greek Scriptures of the New Testament.] We are free to respond: *yes, no, maybe, sometimes, once in a while, "don't know",or "whatever"...* **Grace abounds. It's our choice and our opportunity to question, wonder, reflect, decide. That is the best way to grow and expand!**

My experience is in every challenging difficult welter and waste, *in-the-deep-darkness* circumstance, fear, doubt, with its accompanying pressure to run, hide, feel defeated, abandoned, alone, and helpless **will rise to the surface of our awareness and demand attention.** It will challenge our willingness to believe or embrace this story of creation's possibility. Isn't that what we're here to learn, play with, experiment with, and maybe grow with on a very personal level? **It's a process, not an accomplishment. We all live on *Planet Earth University* to learn what we need to learn!**

Genesis 1:1-2

*"When God began to create heaven and earth and the earth then was welter and waste and darkness over the deep **and** God's breath hovering over the waters,..."*

God's *ruah* -spirit-breath-wind- is HOVERING over the waters. Hovering is a very significant word here. The *Hebrew word* translated as **HOVERING** into English is later found elsewhere in only **one other** significant place in the entire Bible.

Author's Note
Translators commonly find Hebrew words that occur in only one or two places in all of the Hebrew Bible making the job of translating far from an exact science. There is some best guess activity applied here and in many places!

I have placed **the other location** of the word translated as **"Hovering"** in the exact scriptural context below. It is in the 5th "Book of Moses" called Deuteronomy. In this setting it describes an eagle fluttering over its young, and so might have a connotation of giving birth. Here is the text:

Deuteronomy 32:10,11
*"He found him in the wilderness land,
in the waste of the howling desert.
He encircled him, gave mind to him,
watched him like the apple of His eye.
Like an eagle who rouses his nest,
over his fledglings **he hovers,**
He spread His wings, He took him,
He bore him on His pinion."*
                Translation by Robert Alter

By the image of God's spirit-breath *hovering*, **we can imagine an active** *eagle like presence* **that is using its wings to** *rouse* **the nest.** The image of the wind from an eagle's wing blowing out unwanted debris, and stimulating the young eaglets to move, arise, and grow is vivid. TRANSFER THAT IMAGE to **the nature of the breath-presence of God in our lives** providing **both** safety and **rousing stimulation so that we might grow and become more of what we were born to be.** I call that LOVE! Others might think of it as an irritation, a bother, a nuisance. It's up to us to choose.

What is the **most authentic expression of love** for your life? Is love that which compels new growth and new possibility in your life, or is love that which allows you to stay safely and comfortably in the nest until we decide to make a new decision?

Let's step back once again.

We begin with an amazing description of God's *vision* **intending** *to create Heaven and Earth*. This reflects what the story tellers could understand of their whole universe. It was their story of Faith slowly developing over many years and generations. In this story God begins to create with a totally disorganized gathering of useless waste as might be possible in the mind of the storyteller. The story then introduces the one *secret ingredient* that can change every situation in every life or period of history for all time: *the hovering* **breath-presence** *of God.*

In God's creative loving presence new possibility is unexpectedly waiting in the deep darkness, my deep darkness, your deep darkness, the world's deep darkness. In all those times and circumstances when no one can see or know it, God is there, God's **spirit-breath**

is present. The very **intimate personal breath-spirit of God *is hovering*.** If you believe it, or don't believe it, it always stands as a possibility. In this story, the Hebrews' ancient personal story, **this belief stands before us as being *"hammered out on the anvil of their lived experience"* for generation after generation, and by God's Love is offered to all!**

Life Coach Notes:
The **challenging aspect** of God's creative *hovering and rousing* is the *"way-of"*, or manner in which God seems to work. [at least in my life] It is generally not like I might logically expect it to play out. It's rather **mysterious, surprising** and **unexpected.** In my personal experience the recognition of how God's creative *magic* **seems to rouse, hover, or effect me** *is best realized as I reflect on things that have happened in my past.* What about your life? Has any difficult *rousing* squeezed you into becoming a new-better-different person? Have you launched out into the unforeseen with a sense of apprehension only to have things somehow miraculously work out? Have you launched out with high hopes only to have things not work out, and therefore be compelled to retreat, retrace your steps, reflect, and evaluate, which then leads to a newer unanticipated **awareness**, with new **intentions**, and an *even more desirable outcome*? If you have, I suspect it wasn't an **easy** ride along the way. But have you grown?

But Wait, what does "the hovering breath of God" do next in the story?

Genesis 1:1-3 : "When God began to create heaven and earth and the earth then was welter and waste and darkness over the deep and

God's breath hovering over the waters, God said,...

In God's *first action* beyond hovering: *God SPEAKS*.

My earliest education about this story was: 1) God created using **divine speech** as a God's creative tool of choice, and 2) it was from a lofty distance that God summoned creation. The implication was that God was removed from the local arena of creation. That made sense from the point of view of the scholar suggesting it. At that time, I just allowed it to be on my *shelf of explanations* until I became more aware of the details of the story. The details have led me to consider how **amazingly intimate** God's creating process is from my perspective.

Here's my perception and thinking: **Breath** is essential in the lives of all mammals on earth. *Our* very existence on earth depends on breath. Breath is both physical and spiritual at the same time. In the Hebrew language the word **"ruah"** [*presence-spirit]* of God is the **breath** of God. **"Spiritus"** [French] meaning **breath** is another dramatic affirmation that Spirit-breath comes from God and *gives life.* It is **the most intimate presence of God in creation.** God's **spirit-breath** originates from the inner core of God's being like it does in our human bodies. Our chest and heart is the seat of our emotional and biological ***being*** *which both receives and expels the breath of life.* **When our breathing stops our life on earth stops.** When we desire to speak our breath passes over vocal cords which vibrate with sound. We shape the sound into meaning. **When God speaks I believe it is from the depth of God's intimate creative spirit.** God is symbolized through these powerful human metaphors as creating with God's intimate breath and we can learn something about how these Hebrew storytellers experienced and conceived of God. Of course all of this is up to you to decide for yourself. This what makes sense to me.

In this **story of an intimate spiritual creation process** there is much to be learned about God by paying attention to the details. *Just as in the life of a human artist there is much to be learned about the artist by watching her create and noticing the very nature and character of her manifested creations!*

What kind of art does an artist paint? Which colors are chosen? How do the colors come together to give expression? What shapes does a sculpture take at the hands of the artist? What form of creative expression feels best to your soul? At one time in my early 30's I found myself drawn to the natural shapes of pieces of seasoned juniper trees. I would split shapes off from a log and find forms that were pleasing, then glue them together into a larger sculpture. I loved the smell and found the natural shapes amazing. They lifted my spirit into a closer intimacy with God's spirit.

I find it most amazing to watch a 'spray paint' artist create one amazing piece after another. The artist surprises me as he first seems to be making a big mess with his paint, but as I watch what appears to be rapid indiscriminate uncontrolled paint spray swishes and squirts, the image of something amazing begins to take shape. Then with a few more swishes of paint from the spray can a picture of our solar system suddenly appears like magic. Or, the street painter who paints what appears to be a big empty hole on the sidewalk or street only to reveal it is still just the same flat sidewalk or street, but the onlooker would swear there is a big hole in the road surrounded by water! Walk around it! Don't fall in the hole!

I believe the same is true of God's creation as we look at what has naturally occurred over the last many thousands of years. With this idea of creation reflecting back on the creator's soul or spirit I decided that God's favorite colors were blue, green, and brown because that's what I see the most of. Then of course there are the special splashes of many so other colors that come and go with the seasons.

When I was learning about photography one of my teachers taught us how to adjust the camera's light meter to compensate for variations of the color green. He wrote that there were 15,000 shades of green. As a coach-theologian it came to me very clearly that God must enjoy and value diversity! Then I looked up how many species of trees there are on the earth…

God's "Word-Presence-Spirit" is about to do something amazing right before our eyes!

Genesis 1:1-3 : "When God began to create heaven and earth and the earth then was welter and waste and darkness over the deep and God's breath hovering over the waters, God said, "Let there be…"

God's WORD/SPIRIT takes action:

The dictionary offers the **first definition** of "LET" as: *"to cause to; Make."*
However, the **second definition** is more valuable to our emotional/spiritual development: *"to give opportunity to"*, or possibly even the opposite of sorts: *"fail to prevent."* "Letting" or "Allowing" are the critical

"WAYS of God" from this story in the creation of the earth and our human experience. It happens in BOTH *allowing for new possibility* and *allowing things to happen* which may or may not be desirable or pleasant.

Certainly God can **MAKE** as you will discover when reading beyond the first 77 words of Genesis, but I believe there is something critically important in this first phrase as the original authors chose to describe the initial attitude and subsequent *PATTERN* of God's first act of creation: ***"LET there be…"***. All the translations I'm aware of agree on the same English phrase for this first *SPOKEN* action by the "hovering breath/Spirit" of God: ***"Let there be…"***.

Beyond the first 77 words of Genesis, a "LET" precedes each day's creative work. *The emotional mental ATTITUDE of LETTING is the critical attitude which precedes and establishes the climate or condition where something new and amazing* **might be ALLOWED to develop**. That process can be continued each and every day within our own unique lives as we choose to LET, to say Yes!

LIFE COACH NOTES:
God's *style of creating* is an adventure in "allowance." If you're anything like me, my serious adult self is concerned about the danger of allowing/letting things in my life. I've learned over time and experience that caution is my friend and guide. I tend to desire either control or management through education and understanding. So what is the creative deal with LETTING or ALLOWING? Aren't they somewhat dangerous?
I remember myself as a creative child. I remember myself as a creative teenager. I remember myself as an expanding young adult. Certainly I had restrictions but fundamentally *I was cautiously on an adventure of exploration and discovery.* I felt that *allowing creativity*

> *was fun*. I had a garage workshop to explore. I had toys that allowed me to construct. I had excitement in building model airplanes with engines that made them fly. I would explore our encyclopedias to discover animals to draw or sailing ships to admire. And there was the world of girls! The world was full of possibility!

Early on I was unaware of all the things that could **happen** when I tried a new experience. *Life was full of getting an idea, giving it a go, and learning from the experience.* Things might either go wrong or turn out right in any circumstance. For some reason, I most always expected them to go RIGHT. That is, until my experience showed me I had not considered everything involved! God's CREATING new insight and awareness in my life included God's willingness to *"FAIL TO PREVENT"* me from experiencing failure, disappointment or hardship.

Those are the genuine LEARNING EXPERIENCES that brought me to wisdom during my teenage years. I remember an occasion during my 27th year when a member of the congregation I served asked me how I got to be so wise at such a young age. The words that popped out of my mouth were these: "*I started suffering early.*"

Yet I believe God has always attempted to guide, lead, and open my awareness to dangerous possibilities before they occurred, like God does for most of us. I am almost certain that any person who has made it to the age of 18 has experienced at least 5 unrecognized miracles happening in their lives that saved them from serious harm or death.

When I project beyond the limits of just my personal life's creative experiences, I think of the organization which was initially designed and commissioned to be Christ's BODY on EARTH. That would be the ***Church*** within

Christianity in all its hundreds of traditions and organizational systems and styles. The *Church* has over its centuries of evolution **reduced the sacred divine creative "*letting-allowing*"** of God's spirit in the world to an attitude dominated by control, management, structure, and in some circumstances oppression. All of that seems to be the OPPOSITE of the model in this story of **God's hovering spirit breath** simply *letting into becoming.*

As we become committed to the adventure of *allowing* **the guidance of God's Spirit to influence our inner hearts** *through the leadership of our intuition,* we will become amazing creators! *When we can find within our hearts the willingness* **trust** *enough to* **allow/ let** *the Spirit-Breath that is always hovering over our lives to inspire and lead, we will be joining the holy adventure just like all the flawed patriarchs and prophets who have come before.* **When we** *allow* **the guidance of the Creator's Spirit-Breath** be be recognized and accepted, we will soon discover for ourselves who we are as unique individuals. We will discover and own what we genuinely like and don't like regardless of society's expectations. *We will discover and own where the inner heart breath of our unique soul-spirit is fulfilled. We will have a greater sense of what path to follow, what goals to accomplish, and what gifts are in harmony with our inner beings as we offer them in love to the rest of the world.*

Consider for a moment how the characteristic of God *letting* something come into being is in direct contrast to earthly rulers as they go about *ruling*. Earthly rulers *command or order.* The President of the United States can issue a Presidential **order**. It's not a Presidential *letting*. Even Jean-Luc Picard of the Starship Enterprise would say, *"Make it so."*

According to this story, God did NOT command creation to come into existence. God **allowed it to BE**. The story doesn't even use the phrase popular among CRUSADERS of every age and religion desiring to feel as if their decision to act in a certain way or hold a certain value demands divine validation with the phrase, *'God WILLS IT'*. In this story **GOD ALLOWS IT; GOD 'LETS' IT BE.**

Life Coach Notes:
Fear holds, resists, worries, and attempts to control. While learning may take place in either the controlling or allowing. The willingness to *dance on the waves of change* is a lot more fun for the courageous who will risk **allowing**. That attitude also follows the model presented in 3 of the New Testament Gospel accounts of Jesus 'walking on the water' across the sea to the disciples during a storm.

A NEW TESTAMENT GOSPEL STORY [told in my own way]
I have it on good authority -my own- *this is a secret dialogue* not recorded in the Gospel account where Peter walks on the water with Jesus: It seems Jesus has been off by himself praying, and early in the morning he comes walking across the sea to the disciples who are in a fishing boat. They see him and, *"It's a Ghost!!"* erupts from the men in the boat at the sight of Jesus walking on the water. Jesus gets close enough to be fully recognized, then Peter turns to John and Matthew and says, *"Here boys, hold my beer, I want to try something..."* He ASKS permission from Jesus to come to him, and as he steps on to the water, the storm and the wind catch him off guard, and he begins to sink causing him to cry out to Jesus, *"Lord, save me!"* Then Jesus reaches out to him and helps him up and into the boat and says to him, *"You little-faith, why did you doubt?"* Peter replies, *"Give me a break Lord. I'm new at this and I'm still learning, OK!? You know me, I'll probably mess up again in the future!"* I'm pretty sure that's exactly how it REALLY happened.

In this Gospel story, the fundamental characteristic of God as Creator is that God **lets and allows.** I call attention to the presence of God in Jesus as he *heard Peter request* to come to him walking on the water. Jesus *allowed it* without question. Jesus did not caution, or warn, or discourage Peter's desire to come to him across the water. Regardless of your opinion of Jesus or the Greek New Testament, God's **allowance** sets the standard, and provides the foundation where creation might realistically offer the possibility of manifesting *Heaven and Earth.* All that God will create *and especially we who are created as God's children, the offspring of God's love,* is **offered as the free gift of being allowed to experience, allowed to *BE and BECOME*.** This is a super important attitude **because it tells us about the WAY of God.**

Author's Note:
Regardless of your feelings or opinions about Jesus or the stories of his life in the gospel accounts it is important to remember that he was first and foremost **a Jew**. He was reared through the Hebrew scriptures and the core of those texts are the first five books of the Bible.

***The Creation Characteristic of
the WAY of God
is to "LET-'us'-BE-come."***

Genesis 1:1-3 : "When God began to create heaven and earth and the earth then was welter and waste and darkness over the deep and God's breath hovering over the waters,

God said, "Let there be LIGHT." And there was light…"

The *LIGHT* of Eternal and Everlasting **Possibility** has just ***exploded over the void of welter and waste, deep and damp, empty and dark.*** **Everything is now *transformed.*** **God has entered the arena of manifested matter with the first component of its transformation: LIGHT.** I *strongly believe* it is a LIGHT well beyond the limits of the human *visible light spectrum.*

Please consider this question: What was/is the nature and character of the **LIGHT** God created on the very first day?

I suggest that it is far beyond our intellectual awareness, ***but within our intuitive awareness*** of the original story tellers. It is so much more than what modern science has defined as part of the visible light spectrum.

Author's Note
The visible light spectrum is the portion of the total electromagnetic spectrum of light that is visible to the human eye. "Google-it" and you will discover there is much more to the whole spectrum than just the spectrum that is visible to our eyes! While light photons originate from our Sun and the various sources of light on earth, I believe the story tellers of this tale somehow inherently knew to separate God's creation of LIGHT on, "first day" from the creation of the "two great lights, and the stars" they inserted into the story on "fourth day." I believe the nature of the **LIGHT** on this first day is so much more vast than the visible light we might *logically* connect to this first day event.

I remember my awareness of this idea *dawning on me* as I was preparing for a class on Genesis Chapter 1 while teaching a group of adults. Reading down through the story's daily sequence of God's creative *Let-there-be's*, I recognized that the *sun, moon, and stars* were created on **day 4** in the creation sequence. It reads: *"And God said, "Let there be lights in the vault of the heavens to divide the day from the night, and they shall be signs for the fixed times and for days and years,* **and** *they shall be lights in the vault of the heavens to light up the earth."* I then think to myself, *"Myself, I say, there must be something going on here that I have not noticed, been aware of, or ever even thought about before this very moment!"*

The **fourth day's agenda** is totally separated from the first day's *letting of the **light***, and to my mind obviously aligned with another important aspect of creation: God establishing ORDER and MEANING out of the chaos -welter and waste- from which everything has emerged. This ORDER will extend to **measured time allowing rituals and social practices to be followed.** This enables human existence to be ordered in a manner that supports prosperity, stability, and a culture's social/religious practices, all of which are connected to emotional health and prosperity.

God has intentionally chosen to give the opportunity for *the LIGHT to Be created* as the first act within the previous *realm of total DARKNESS*. *This establishes a CONTRAST of options and choices: darkness or light, and one will never exclude or banish the other.* **In this first act of creation the condition of contrast and the possibility of *choice* is now established by virtue of what is available.** Before there was only *welter waste and darkness over the deep*. Like in, *"No choices here ma'am, there is only darkness."* Now there is all of that, and another option: **LIGHT**!!

HOWEVER, God's LIGHT is MORE than we may have ever imagined at our first awareness using common sense or analytical thought!

NEW TESTAMENT GOSPEL
In John's Gospel of the Greek testament, John writes in Chapter 1: "What has come into being (4) in him was life, and the life was the **LIGHT** of all people. (5) The **LIGHT** shines in the darkness, and the darkness did not overcome it. (6) There was a man sent from God, whose name was John. (7) He came as a witness to testify to the **LIGHT**, so that all might believe through him. (8) He himself was not the **LIGHT**, but he came to testify to the **LIGHT**. (9) **The true LIGHT, which enlightens everyone**, was coming into the world.
         New Revised Standard Version of the Bible.
John 1:3b-9a

The author of the John's Gospel is referring to **much more than either the visible light spectrum or EVEN the entire scope of the electromagnetic spectrum!** Like all sacred text, the language of symbolism and metaphor points beyond itself to a truth in abstract reality existing beyond the provable, measurable, observable tangibility of our material world or life.

Author's Note: *If my mother, "bless her heart", were reading this she would look up from that sentence with a puzzled look on her face. The part of her brain that perceived abstract concepts and imagined their potential implications for everyday life was -in my opinion- under developed in favor of the left side of her brain that was super smart regarding details, sequence, order, and discipline. That part of her left brain was highly developed for perceiving the world of details and all their array within the tangible world of matter and substance. But while she might not have been able to conceptualize abstract relationships **she was guided by Spirit in her own way.** I'm thankful for that and for God's creative LIGHT which can guide all of us beyond our own limited vision, perspective, or perception! So let's explore the possibilities together!*

Consider for a moment the spiritual traditions and philosophy of Hinduism and Buddhism.
One of the guiding principles or goals of both these traditions has to do with achieving *En**light**enment*

through inner reflection-meditation. The term *enLIGHTENment* is for me a revealing connection to the origin of **LIGHT** whereby **all people** might gain intimate spiritual connection to the Source of Creation through God's very first act of creation: *"Let there be Light..."*

 **CONSIDER THESE WITNESSES TO THE LIGHT OF SPIRIT EXISTING BEYOND THE ELECTROMAGNETIC SPECTRUM:**

"I wandered so aimless, life filled with sin
I wouldn't let my dear savior in
Then Jesus came like a stranger in the night
*Praise the Lord, I saw the **light***
*I saw the light, I saw the **light***
No more darkness, no more night
Now I'm so happy no sorrow in sight
*Praise the Lord, I saw the **light**."*
Hank Williams Sr. 1948
public domain

Hank Williams Sr., a sensitive creative spirit, lived and died at 29 years of age with an addiction to alcohol that interrupted the function of his brain neurons, but still, I fully believe he did see and experience the **light**. He was inspired to write this song by a remark his mother made when arriving in Montgomery, Alabama as they returned from a concert.

*"This **little light** of mine*
I'm going to let it shine
*Oh, this **little light** of mine*
I'm going to let it shine
*This **little light** of mine*
I'm going to let it shine
Let it shine, all the time, let it shine."
Traditional gospel song meant for children

written by Harry Dixon Loes in the 1920s.
public domain

The LIGHT of each person's Spirit Connection reflects the LIGHT Source of their personal creation. In my professional years, there were periods of time when I had the opportunity to serve as a song leader for pre-school children. I have witnessed time and time again in the children's attitude and expressions a pure *spirit light* filling the room while they were singing This Little Light of Mine. As younger children can easily do, they would emotionally embrace the LIGHT within their spirits. It was the LIGHT with which they were born that shined undimmed by the realities of their lived experience. Their JOY sang without knowing a thing about what they were doing other than **singing** and celebrating in the ***LIGHT of their created existence!***

"You fill up my senses, like a night in a forest; like the mountains in springtime, like a walk in the rain; like a storm in the desert, like a sleepy blue ocean; you fill up my senses, come fill me again…" Annie's Song by John Denver 1973

While John Denver did not mention LIGHT in this song I believe the LIGHT of Spirit was manifested in his experience and reflected in both the lyric, the melody, and the waltz time of this song. He wrote it ***in his mind*** during the time it took the main chair lift at Aspen Mountain, Colorado, to get to the top of his ski run. It was a little over 10 minutes. He had just completed an exhilarating and challenging ski run down a very difficult slope, and the sense of total immersion in the beauty of the colors and sounds that filled all his senses on the ride back up the mountain inspired him to think about the beauty of the earth and his love for his wife Annie. He composed the lyrics in that short span of time! Later she would write that he skied down the mountain, following the lift ride up, came home, and wrote the song down on paper.

She also shared what I consider to be THE critical *[almost essential?]* ingredient *originating from his personal experience just prior* to his decision to go to the ski mountain that morning. They had been struggling with their relationship, and had come to a successful resolution. John's response was to head over to the ski mountain for a few celebration runs.

Life Coach Notes:
In my experience **the Light** of imagination and creativity can sometimes be born as an extension of the dynamic contrast between our feelings of *Darkness* when struggling with a difficult but valuable relationship, and the the feelings of *Light* when coming to some sense of new awareness or hope. As we faithfully reflect, work, and wait in darkness we automatically hope to discover a WAY for the **Light** to be allowed into our experience. *Inward Sight* **lights up** new possibilities like a silent spirit dove *alighting on the* **inner awareness** *of our heart and mind:*
    "Now I see the LIGHT!"

Experience the LIGHT of Imagination and Creativity

Isn't that the nature of **in-*sight***? The struggle, the focused work, and the *groping around in the dark* for a solution in those circumstances where we want life to be different, or better, or brighter? Sometimes a difficult, complex problem needing to be solved is somehow intimately connected to the possibility of experiencing a brilliant LIGHT of insight leading to a solution. Our challenge is to stay faithful in the darkness and work toward the Light. God has a *way* beyond our foreseeable awareness to lead us into the **LIGHT** even though when we arrive we are sometimes frightened far beyond our comfort zones.

The LIGHT of Insight

Both **insight** and **understanding** seem to be part of the experience of **allowing an experience** in which the first created **Light** may reveal itself into our awareness. Sometimes we think it is OUR brilliant idea. We are really part of the team as we co-create with God's Spirit. I believe seeing the **LIGHT** is much more of a *creative partnership* between our **Light** and God's **LIGHT**.

THIS IS ONE WAY IT HAS HAPPENED IN MY LIFE. It was the Guiding LIGHT of Hope and Trust beyond logic's awareness.

I've been married twice. My first marriage came when I was a young inexperienced 21 year old.

At 19, I was like many young men of my era who had very little experience in the difficult practical life experiences that teach us so much through suffering. When I met the woman who would become my first wife I was attempting to recover from my break up from a previous *first love's* mutually passionate year long relationship. There was no one in my life to help me reflect and process the pain of the breakup, therefore, like so many of us, I was just doing the best I could. I felt and acted as if I had *let the pain go*. Repress it and move forward was the best I could do.

I understood why she broke up with me. I couldn't be *mad* at her. She was 16, a junior in high school, very cute, and sensual. I was 19, a sophomore in college and 100 miles away. She didn't *play me*, she just gave me back the necklace I had given her. I had no idea the unresolved pain from that break up would silently and powerfully compel me to choose a person to marry who was the **safe** polar opposite from the passionate young girl of my break up. My emotional wound was guiding my choices, and come to find out those choices would lead me into a 10 year long *practical education experience* in marriage, fatherhood, self awareness, and finally the decision to claim a new set of possibilities for my life that would take me out of my marriage, and into alignment with my deepest core desires through the **guiding Light of my inner heart.**

My inner **heart-self** that gratefully lives in the LIGHT beyond my intellectual ability to comprehend had been working and struggling for an extended time attempting to try every tactic and tool of relationship building to make my first marriage be what I needed. One of those tactics was to ask less of my marriage for the intimacy I wanted, and to redirect that spirit into working in various camp settings with other adults who teamed up to help early teens begin to discover who they were within the loving and accepting arms of God's SPIRIT. It functioned well for about 6 years. One day during year 6 of this journey while driving alone on a very slow Ford tractor ferrying camp equipment along an empty county road in western Oklahoma I began to weep. I didn't know it at the time, but I was leaving my marriage. I just knew I was deeply sad, sad, sad. My inner soul had been working on the condition of my inner heart's darkness for some time, and it was finally time to come out into the Light. It took a week of reflection on what was going on inside me before I was absolutely clear I was not going to continue in my marriage. I had no idea what would happen after getting out, but I knew **out** held the possibility for a hell-of-a-lot more **LIGHT** than staying **in**. I had stayed in for 10 long years. My guidance was clear. I would begin my quest to really be married the way I wanted to an appropriate life partner, but first I had to move out.

That quest led to meeting and marrying the perfect woman. A marriage in which we had both previously made the aggressive move to be the decision makers who left our first marriages to find more. Our commitment since that time has been to grow and become more while living as best as possible within the LIGHT of our personal lives as individuals, and by joining the light-synergy of our companionship with each other in partnership with the Origin of LIGHT. We've just begun the 45th year of our experience together. And, by the way, having a relationship with one's **self** and with another **self** requires a lot of attention to **self, each other,** AND **the relationship.** "You gotta work it baby!" It is VERY rewarding work!

The LIGHT is a manifested spirit extension of God's Love breath presence.

Love and the Creator's LIGHT are married. They are lovers known to one another.
When we sit alone looking outside ourselves, or while waiting for love, we live in hope. There is something inside us that holds a spark of **Light** even when we're physically alone in the dark, because that is exactly the circumstance described in this very first story in the Bible. ***God's breath hovers over every deep darkness, and we can only trust in the love that will eventually speak: "Let there be Light." RIGHT?!***

Life Coach Notes:
As I mentioned earlier, the tool that has helped me learn to trust and believe in God's LIGHT is this:
I have reflected on my personal experience/journey by looking back for examples from my life on the many occasions upon which I received help from unreasonable, unexpected, unearned, irrational, illogical, and mysterious sources, *and asked myself this/these question(s):*

-When were occasions in my past when I was cared for by something I did NOT expect, or could not have anticipated? I made a list.
-When did I get help from a totally unseen source? I made a list.
-When was I offered an opportunity I did not either anticipate or seek? I made a list.
-When did I have experiences that revealed a new aspect of my life I had not previously been aware of? I made a list.
*-When have I had an experience another person might call **luck**, or **chance**, or when I have thought, "That just came out-of-the-blue?" I believe that is significant. I keep a list.*
*When a list compiled from personal experience confronts our conscious awareness, the physical awareness that I/you/we receive help from **outside** ourselves, it can provide a firm basis for moving forward in hope.*
I then can keep my attention on the guidance of my inner spirit as expressed through my desires. That is my compass.
*While we cannot control what may happen **to** us, we can in some manner control how we **choose to think about** our experiences and what we name them.*

Because of God's *Letting*, Light has and will continue to shine in our darkness. Before God's Light, darkness was the only option, now we can choose!

I invite you to consider this idea: **YOU are the Light.** This is a statement of possibility. It is an AWARENESS of **your valuable state of being.** It has NOTHING to do with authority or power or status in Earth consciousness. It is simply a statement of fact that you have been created and born into an *Earth-form* as a Creature who breathes the Spirit-Breath of the Holy Divine Creator of LIGHT, and therefore you embody the **Light from that creator in your UNIQUE way**. Period. *"Now, what-R-you gonna do with it?"*

Genesis 1:1-4 : "When God began to create heaven and earth and the earth then was welter and waste and darkness over the deep and God's breath hovering over the waters, God said, "Let there be LIGHT." And there was Light. And God saw the light, that it was good, ..."

God sees the LIGHT, and announces it was GOOD.

God creates, then evaluates the creative act. Isn't that the pattern for everyone who is a creator? Whether it is a new outfit for a special occasion, or a new idea regarding the arrangement of a room in the house, we act on our creative insight then decide how we feel about it. We do something we hope will make a desirable difference and then evaluate the results. In this story God evaluates God's own work. This is a characteristic pattern of God's creative process that is consistent throughout the remainder of Chapter 1, and can be seen scattered throughout all of Genesis.

As God's creatures, we humans share characteristics of our loving parent/creator. We create, evaluate, and decide how we feel about what we've done. A very appropriate similarity to the Creator!

But wait, there's more: **God is making a powerful statement of *value and practice*** we might put on our refrigerator door: ***"THE LIGHT IS GOOD! IT'S GOD APPROVED"*** The **LIGHT** of insight, the **light** of awareness, the **light** of truth, the **light** of inspiration, the **light** leading from wisdom, and the **light** that brings about constructive change; all of these are **good**. **Naming them *good* is a choice God models for us.** What you call them changes their reality and power in our lives.

WELL, EXCEPT, *we have another option*! There is a contrasting view of the world and how to live in it. In the Greek "New Testament" the writer of the Gospel of John reported in chapter 3 that Jesus said:

*"**19** And this is the judgment, that **the light has come into the world**, and **men loved darkness rather than light**, because their deeds were evil. **20** For every one who does evil hates the **light**, and does not come to the **light**, lest his deeds should be exposed. **21** But he who does what is true comes to the **light**, that it may be clearly seen that his deeds have been wrought in God.*

Consider the earthly creators/leaders you know, *[and if we are to be honest with ourselves, maybe you and me from time to time?]* especially in politics, but even in business practices will not, and sometimes cannot affirm that **"light is good"**. Many operate from the value that too much LIGHT on any subject is undesirable. They want to **keep others in the dark** about certain things.

Consider the practice of social media tracking its users' desires, practices, habits, patterns, and choices, AND choosing to keep those practices and their information **hidden in the darkness** from those whom they are tracking. The practices of keeping political constituents, employees, customers, people in general in the **dark** and away from the awareness of issues and aspects of life that affect them is a choice made multiple times each day. I doubt those who make the decisions toward darkness would agree that **LIGHT IS GOOD**. What do you think?

Some people *carry a story about love* which tells them they should keep the people they love **in the dark** regarding painful information of many kinds. There seems to be an underlying hope people they love might be saved from the emotional weight or burden of that particular sorrow, pain, or sadness. When we adopt this position we have made a statement about our own lack of trust in our loved one's ability or inability to deal with the **light of truth** - *that they are too weak to deal with the truth,* and *in love we must protect them from painful truth.* When I am honest with myself in those circumstances, **I am the one I am hoping to be protected** from watching *them* suffer at the prospect of their sadness that someone they love is experiencing suffering. The actual reality is that everyone WILL EVENTUALLY FIND OUT.

I believe the important question to ask is, *"**What might it mean to trust ourselves and them with the light of the truth,** and then stand together in loving support of one another as we all grieve, struggle, and adjust?"* **The Holy Divine Light** will be there with us. It always is when we have the willingness to be aware and seek its **LIGHT**.

Life Coach Notes:
*On occasions when I feel insecure or vulnerable about revealing something, and recognize I want to hide myself in the dark from the potential criticism of others, it can be a very helpful time to stop and ask myself a question: **"So, what's the deal here, Phil?"** The subjects, arenas, and aspects of my life in which I might prefer darkness will actually **reflect a light of insight back on me**, helping identify my insecurities and fears. What I've learned about hiding those aspects of my inner life **is this: it is a powerful revealer of***

truth. It requires courage to see, explore, understand, and embrace the Light that shines on the condition of my inner being. When I understand the issues involved I can make a much better decision regarding how to relate to them. What makes them difficult is their interconnectedness to multiple issues and aspects that do not easily allow obvious simple answers leading to clean or acceptable solutions. Life is almost always MESSY.
The Light will transform the darkness and its accompanying fear once courage brings the **Light to reveal and guide** the issues needing a solution. Trusting that reality is sometimes challenging and almost always important!

Genesis 1:1-4 : "When God began to create heaven and earth and the earth then was welter and waste and darkness over the deep and God's breath hovering over the waters, God said, "Let there be LIGHT." And there was Light. And God saw the light, that it was good, and God divided the light from the darkness,..."

This ancient story holds that in the beginning darkness was the only condition of "the Earth then." As God **allowed Light**, there was a new option that came into being, and divided the darkness. **God's intent is to allow Light to be the contrast to the darkness.** Darkness has not been somehow *destroyed or banned* from creation. The ancients telling the story innately knew that bringing light into the darkness was important because when our circumstance is either all darkness or all light, things are incomplete and out of the balance brought through perspective.

The ancient story tellers inherently recognized the rhythms of both our physical life and our emotional life on Earth, and told a story about God's awareness that **if** life was to prosper there needed to be a contrasting rhythm between light and dark, expansion and contraction, rest and expenditure. Modern science will affirm that both humans and the natural world need darkness as well as light for our physical and emotional health. One of the growth challenges we face in dealing with the 24/7 availability of human created light is the degree that our day-night rhythms become distorted and out of balance, adding stress to both our emotional and physical *bodies*.

While this story doesn't address the origins of darkness, it allows darkness to exist without setting it up as the destructive evil force in a morality tale of an evil empire. Darkness in this story is not out to conquer and control everything and everyone through totalitarian methods. **In this story darkness is just an original condition into which light has been created and added;** however, in my mind that is the perfect metaphor for something more about our human experience.

It is *in our spiritual/emotional life* that we begin to associate the physical circumstance of darkness with a negative. For good reason. We know that in physical darkness we can't see. We sometimes stumble in the darkness. We more easily get lost or disoriented in the darkness. Sometimes people whose intent is to harm or take advantage of other people use the darkness to hide their schemes. I have used the phrase, *"I'm in the dark about that"* when I don't have the information I need to solve a problem. I need insight from the Light.

When we move to change our blind vulnerable situations or to reveal the hurtful actions of others, *we shine a Light* on the stumbling blocks. We uncover the plot to steal and destroy. It is therefore easy *[or natural?]* to set up an attitude of conflicting contrast between the spiritual *Light* of God's first act of creation *and* the descriptive pre-existing contrast of *welter and waste, formless void, and deep darkness* to which Light has been *allowed*.

This story is the absolute foundation upon which we humans might understand and discover the value of **our personal Light** in the experiences provided through being born [incarnated] from Spirit into an *earth-form human* body. At our physical birth we begin a life-long - *regardless how long or brief in "earth time" that life may be* - journey to experience, struggle, grow, live, embrace, and *become* through every experience in each day's living. Each day will be another opportunity for experiences **in the process of becoming more** as Spiritual Beings living in an earthly body here on *Planet Earth University*.

This Genesis story is that **LIGHT is always available** in the *welter&waste, formless void* of emotional and spiritual darkness. **God's breath hovers! That is *THIS story*.**

The night I decided to leave the United Methodist Church and possibly the ministry all together was **another one of those experiences of darkness**. The Methodist Church [before it became the United Methodist Church] was my spiritual mother. It was the place I received care from a big loving family. It was a place I could call home. It was mostly a place of nurture and acceptance. It was a most influential part of my growing up.

This is my story. In the depression years just preceding WWII, my parents had moved to town after having been reared and married in a rural setting. They knew if they wanted to meet people and make new friends they just needed *to go to church*. When my brother and I were born -*8 years apart*- they brought us to church in our turn. I was bashful, shy, and somewhat insecure. As I aged, I soon found church to **be the place** where I received love, had fun, found meaning, and *experienced a home* in which to ***grow*** and ***expand***. I was in Sunday school beginning as a pre-schooler when my mom was one of my teachers, then elementary through the 5th grade. As a 6th grader, I became part of the youth group. I felt very special. It was perfect for me. Throughout middle school and high school I came into my own as a responsible older teen taking on more adult roles in the church. My first year in college I lived at home and participated in a *college and career* group for young adults. Centenary Methodist Church was **my** place to **become**. I went to Church camp every summer throughout Jr High and High School, and carried an identity with my school friends as a *church kid*. A little embarrassing for an adolescent boy, but I had so many *manly things* in my life that I could handle their limiting categories. Even then I didn't fit cultural stereotypes.

While I had dreams of being a fighter pilot in the Air Force, I knew nothing about exactly how to do it, and at 17 I suddenly found myself drawn into preparing for the professional ministry. There was an internal *guiding spirit* that led me to feel a *sense of light* in the idea that I could help people, and I had grown up with the experience that *the church was the place to help people feel loved.* My *inner heart felt a glow of Light* when I thought about working for God through the church. I attended and graduated from a Methodist University, worked as a youth director in a Methodist Church during my last 3 years at the university, and attended a Methodist seminary following graduation. Following seminary I worked as an associate pastor in a United Methodist Church in an urban area for 3 years, then pastored two small churches as a lead pastor for 3 years. I then moved to another suburban church as an associate pastor during which time I got a divorce, and was assigned to another church as lead pastor. That's when I met Diana who would become my wonderful wife-lover-partner. We had a child together, and I was assigned to be the lead pastor in a county seat farm community. That's when I finally came to an end with my desire and ability to work professionally in the church. I share the story as my living testimony to the **Spirit-Light** that comes even in the deepest darkness.

We had been married four and a half years, and were working very diligently on our marriage. We were the parents of yours, mine, and ours [4 children], the pastor of a fairly large church in a culture that was socially and theologically disconnected from where I was or wanted to be.

In my experienced lucidity of the character and nature of the United Methodist constitutional system of hierarky and the moving of pastors and their families where and when the bishop and his cabinet thought they should go, and when he/they didn't have a way to spend the time to know my character and ability as a unique human being, it became too much to bear. I was led into a congregational setting that was so unhealthy I could realize I had to change. But of course, like most significant events of this kind, I was so totally immersed in the struggle *to make everything work in a life-giving manner* that I *didn't realize how exhausted my spirit* had become.

One night after we had been in this county seat church for about about 2 years my wife and I were going through a stressful and critical discussion regarding our marriage, and I thought to myself that If I were to lose her and our daughter my world would be covered by a black curtain. I was laying on a couch while they were in another room while she was thinking about her life, and I saw a black curtain close before my face as I laid on the couch. I saw **nothing but darkness** before my eyes. **My strong inner soul** said, *"Phil even if they were to leave you should at least have your life's work and your life's purpose to give you guidance and joy, and honestly, **you HATE this job!**"* **THAT WAS IT! My truth was realized!** That was ALL I needed. I may be slow but I'm not stupid! I got up from the couch, found my wife, and told her we were leaving the church and maybe the ministry. That was the beginning of another amazing growth phase in my life, our lives as a married couple, and the life of our family.

LIGHT shining in my DARKNESS.
Creation, Creation, ever evolving Creation.

Genesis 1:1-5 : "When God began to create heaven and earth and the earth then was welter and waste and darkness over the deep and God's breath hovering over the waters, God said, "Let there be LIGHT." And there was Light. And God saw the light, that it was good, and God divided the light from the darkness. And God called the light Day, and the darkness He called Night."

In this sentence of creation's "first day," **God names** the light **day** and the darkness She **names night**. What a wise and helpful act. God's **naming is a pattern of creation** that began immediately following the assessment of the **condition of "the earth then"** and the creation of **Light**.

One of the first things we humans learn when we want to get something accomplished is to start by **naming** or *identifying the components* of the situation or circumstance. When we come upon a location where we desire to build something like a home that will support and sustain human life *"in the **Way** of heaven and earth"* as the story says, *we **first aim to establish an orderly foundation***. Earth is a place of matter. Its very nature is that of *tangibility*. I don't know about you, but when I encounter a mess in the garage or a mess in my relationships I first must recognize and **name the characteristics of the *mess*.** You know, the awareness of *seeing the Light* in the situation reveals its identity or condition, *then we claim it by naming it.*

The authors of this ancient story understood the importance of a name in the process of establishing a manageable situation. A consistent quality found in this story throughout this first account of creation as it unfolds through the end of chapter 1 reveals God's practice of continually **naming things**. Naming gives us a tool to bring identity and order to the greater world around us. God is modeling for all time the importance of *naming*, OR the authors of this story recognized that naming was critical in their lives and ascribed this characteristic to God. What does it matter? *The truth is* that somewhere deep inside our psyches there is a strong compulsion to give names to everything from a man's favorite rifle [1950's Disney 'Davy Crockett named his rifle *"Ol Betsy"*] to cars, and an endless assortment of things that mean something to those who use and own them. Have you ever seen pictures of WWII B-17 bomber aircraft that flew in Europe? Names and artwork abound!

I've cooperated on the process of naming 3 children, multiple pets, and two of my 9 -*over the last 50 years*- motorcycles. When I worked as an adult leader with early teens *[middle schoolers]* at summer church camps one of the aspects of their development we attempted to address had to do with their *emerging identity*. A game we played invited them to *list several names* other than their own they would choose to call themselves if they could change their names. It usually stimulated interesting conversation if they knew the reason behind the name their parents gave them, and why they chose the new name they would desire. Identity is reflected in names.

"God called the light Day, and the darkness He called Night."

AUTHOR'S NOTE:
The Mirriam-Webster dictionary definition for **"Day"** is, *"the time of Light between one night and the next"*. Its definition for **"Night"** is, *"the time from dusk to dawn when no sunlight is visible"*. A more contemporary science-like *definition of Day* is a little different: **A Day** is, *"a 24 hour unit of time, reckoned from one midnight to the next, corresponding to a rotation of the earth on its axis."* Reflect on these two definitions for the same reality and then consider that the ancient Hebrews would have understood the first definition, *but would have had NO reference point for understanding the second.* Those realities must be taken into account when reading *any part of the Bible, and especially these first stories.*

Speaking of *names*, and we are you know, you may or may not have noticed this is the first time in Genesis we have encountered a *masculine pronoun* used to reference God; *"...and the darkness HE called Night."* Here's the deal. The issue here is so much more than an issue of *political correctness or sexism*. **We humans need a WAY to relate to God in a form that *allows and nurtures a sense of intimacy*. Personal pronouns afford that bridge.**

Because **males controlled civilization** by brute force for so many thousands of years, and because males were in control of interpreting and writing down the oral narrative that became the written Bible, and because males used their natural aggression and physical strength to generally dominate physically weaker females and males keeping them subservient to male dominance, most references to God are masculine. While masculine references have a place, in isolation they are very ***incomplete, inadequate, and restrictive*** when dealing with both the vast and yet intimate nature of God. With our natural tendency to associate what we understand from our perspective of gender involved with life on earth males project those masculine images to the Holy Divine Creator of the Universe. When we limit our views of God to those earth bound categories we distort and reduce our understanding of God to **level** that severely limits our understanding. You and I, and as necessarily self centered individuals are challenged to grow into the truth that **God is so much more** than the limitations earth-bound categories can reflect.

For example, the struggle to expand our understanding of God can be seen the factual history of how we have perceived and understood the Earth in relationship to the other observable planets in what we now know is *our solar system.* The very name solar system is a perspective that the Sun is the center of a system of planets that are held by gravity to orbits that circle the Sun *comprising a solar system.* In the year 1543 of the Common Era the established Roman church in the West commonly understood that the Earth was the center of all things and that the sun, moon, stars, and all observable objects orbited around the Earth. There had been discrepancies for hundreds of years in observations regarding how these objects circled the earth, but that was just because *they hadn't figured out the patterns yet!*

Then the astronomer Copernicus brought everything into perspective. He determined by observation that *the Earth was not the center of the universe,* and therefore the world and its place in the Church's story of how God placed the Earth at the center of all created things required new understanding, growth, and expansion. The perspective of the previous 2000+ years was wrong. Everything was much more complex than the Christian Church of his day was willing to accept. He and Galileo suffered because of it. Copernicus died after his paper was published, but Galileo was persecuted and put under house arrest for the remainder of his life because his new story about the nature of God and God's creation was a threat to the established order.

So this is an opportunity to consider **WHY** the **CHARACTERISTIC(s) of God** -*[do you remember the Compass Questions?]*- are important. **Discovering characteristics** that are more *comprehensive and authentic* is valuable to our growth as humans attempting to relate to the Holy Divine Creator Source. It's also important to claim and use language that might enable us to feel a more inclusive intimacy toward "**That Which Is Beyond all Earthly Categories,"** and is at the very same time the personal intimate **Holy Breath** that fills our earthly bodies with *life and spirit.*

I believe we are given the grace to make reference to God **by using the gender of the personal pronoun *that best supports our intimate personal relationship with God.*** God's love is intimately PERSONAL. I encourage us to use the *he-she/him or her* that brings us into a warmer, closer relationship to the Holy Divine Creator-Lover.

AUTHORS'S NOTE:
If you are a Christian you will recognize God came in human form as a male because in my opinion God wanted his best chance to be

taken seriously by first century humans. [value the context!] The clear picture I have from the stories of Jesus in all 4 Gospel accounts indicates he behaved as a **human within the perfect balance of the masculine and the feminine within his male body JUST AS He was the Holy and the Human in perfect balance.** My personal feelings are strongly negative toward most of the writers of the remainder of the Greek scriptures - New Testament - because THEY were **first century males** who had NO SENSE of the value of the feminine within the church even though a powerful leadership pattern was set by many of the women in the early church demonstrating they were absolutely critical to the early church's survival and success. As long as I was in professional ministry, women have been the back bone, **and the neck,** of the institutional church. They hold it up and turn the heads of the males who attempt to guide it.

Life Coach Notes: I desire to draw your attention to day 6 of creation in this story. In it you will discover God's words being reported as saying, *"Let us make a human in our image, by our likeness, to hold sway…"* [verse 26]. Then following [in verse 27] *"And God created the human in his image, in the image of God He created him, male and female He created them."* From the fullness that is a multidimensional-both-genders-and-beyond God, there is in **this STORY** the creation of **both male and female at the same time**, and without any prospect of one dominating the other; one being first and the other second. We discover both male and female, masculine and feminine, coming from the **center of God's creativity.** *Think about it.* From the **one source that is God's spirit both** genders, **both** complimentary components, **both** contrasting elements in which we are all held and through which we all have the opportunity to grow together.

Additionally, the term ***"LET US"*** is interpreted by some scholars as an early period in Hebrew culture when they had yet to decide that Elohim was just "One God", because **ALL the surrounding cultures** had multiple Gods. Other Christians will speculate that "LET US" was a reference to God the Father, Jesus the Son, and the Holy Spirit [comprising the Holy Trinity] who were present from the beginning, and making up a **God Council** of sorts comprising the "US"! Or, Or, Or, there is always an "Or" of speculation supporting many perspectives! Your choice. Any person or group leading you to believe there is **only one way**, is **not to be trusted** to reflect healthy understanding the nature of God.

Consider Names of God:
In 1982 Christian recording artist Amy Grant performed a song written by Michael Card and John Thompson that included some of the names of God found in the Hebrew scriptures in the lyric. Here are some of the words:

> *"El shaddai, el shaddai,*
> *El-elyon na adonia,*
> *Age to age you're still the same,*
> *By the power of the name.*
> *El shaddai, el shaddai,*
> *Erkamka na adonai,*
> *We will praise and lift you high,*
> *El shaddai."*

THANK YOU SCHOLARS for this awareness of the significance of the variety of names for God in the text. It came from scholars whose entire lives were focused on the study of scripture. Reading the text closely DAY after DAY, they began to notice all the different names used for **God** in the Hebrew text, and began to associate the usage of certain names with *unique characteristic literary styles and content* from the authors who used that certain name for God. **The scholars did not "make this stuff up," they just described what they discovered in the text itself!** The original authors that use *Elohim* as God's name tell stories that reflect a focus on ritual and order like maybe the Priests of early Judaism would have been interested in using to reflect their bias toward those characteristics that support religious and cultural practices. The references to God as *El Shaddai* might have reflected people wanting to invoke God's all *sufficient power* in a life situation where they felt fear or vulnerability, or possibly during a time of war. In the next book I write on the Second Creation Story *[Genesis 2:4 and following]* the name used for God is **YHWH Elohim.** It is translated as the **Lord God** and brings a **strong picture of intimacy** to the nature and activity of God. None of this can be proven because the words are ancient and the stories preceded the development of writing.

The actual **Hebrew name** in the text being translated as **GOD in this chapter** is *"Elohim"*. In the book of Genesis each time you see the English term **"God"** being used it is this Hebrew word *"Elohim"*. *Throughout the book of Genesis the specific translated name for God signals a detailed shift in the story teller's view of God's character and quality.* I pay attention to those things as important clues of meaning.

This gives us an opportunity to open our understanding of how names reflect something **much more than just** *a way to identify or draw attention to* **something unique** that is similar but not the same. **There** *is a unique identity to the characteristics of God* **from the viewpoint of the storytellers and their perspectives.**

The names they called God might give us a better sense after meaning we might apply to our own lives. **God is so vast and great-expansive that She/He appears in the most appropriate WAY to care for the unique individual lives and experiences in which we humans find ourselves throughout our life times.**

IN A DEEPER LOOK INTO THE CRITICAL IMPORTANCE OF IDENTIFYING and NAMING beyond just identity, please consider the process of *"INTROSPECTIVE NAMING"* from research done by Brene Brown:
*"… a huge part of the **mythology around emotion** is that if we look it - [emotion] - in the eye, we give **it** power…*

the reality is,- [however] - if we look it in the eye, AND NAME IT, it gives us power."

Sociologist
Brene Brown on Instagram

Life Coach Notes:
When something happens between my wife and I that creates an emotional issue of some sort coming between us, my first rule is to stop, reflect, question, examine, and *hopefully discover what values or characteristics are at play* in **both of our lives** that led to or created the issue. My goal in those situations is to identify what unspoken, unrecognized, and sometimes fearful/threatening feelings are at play between us? **Things never happen in a vacuum, and they are rarely someone's FAULT!** They come about because we are unique people with many feelings from a variety of circumstances and experiences that change and evolve within us. In order to assess and discover what needs to be done or adjusted, one must learn to settle, reflect, and do the best we can to **name the components discovered in the process of reflection.** Then we can *let-allow* [the Light of insight], **to shine on that which we have discovered, are able to name, and then OFFER its new insight to us.** It may lead to better understanding, a solution, or new attitude, therefore providing continuing growth in our relationship.
By naming these sometimes subtle but powerful feelings *we have a way to recognize, understand, bring order to, and manage* the essence of what we have found. At that point we may be able to focus on it clearly, and to adopt an appropriate life-giving relationship with it.

Genesis 1:1-5 : "When God began to create heaven and earth and the earth then was welter and waste and darkness over the deep and God's breath hovering over the waters, God said, "Let there be LIGHT." And there was Light. And God saw the light, that it was good, and God divided the light from the darkness. And God called the light Day, and the darkness He called Night. And it was evening and it was morning,…

This eight word sentence completing the first and most meaningful beginning of God's creating of heaven and earth from the void of welter and waste is a **perfect witness to the creative flow of earth-life's rhythms.**

There is a never ending RHYTHM and FLOW to life… (until it all stops of course!). *"And it was evening and it was morning,…"* is a remarkable witness to the movement of light and dark that marks and measures the rhythms and flow of life. We all need the perspective of observation discerning the rhythms of life to give us perspective on flow. This line in the creation story marks that awareness.

We have a 10 year old female German Shepherd Dog who has a great sense of time. She knows when it is time for us to feed her, time for her meds, or time for the family to go to bed. In the morning when she arises, she is ready for a treat biscuit, then as she sees me wash her breakfast food bowl she heads out to her bed to wait. If I become distracted taking too much time she will come back in and stare at me until I regain focus on making her breakfast. After breakfast she has one med she gets in mid morning. Did I mention she doesn't like meds of any kind! She knows when they're coming and leaves the house so we must call her in and shut the back door so she will submit. At dinner time she will come and find me. Mark your clock, it's 5:30. Then there is required *play* *time* the second my wife and I sit down to watch tv after dinner. And finally, about 10 PM she arises from the nap she's been taking for the previous 2 hours to go stand by the treat container on the cabinet because she is ready to get her treat and go to her bed for the evening. She doesn't read either analogue or digital clocks. *[Or does she!?]* I believe *she is like so many of God's creatures and has an internal sense of timing that comes with being in natural alignment with the source of her creator.*

There have been times in my own life when I was so caught up in my work while attempting to help a downtown congregation of traditional Christians that I lost track of my evenings and mornings. My sense of mission pushed me out of my sense of rhythm. I won't go into a long *dog and pony show* about my daily routine holding too many opportunities with too much *warrior focus*, and not enough perspective, but I will tell you the occasion on which I finally *realized the condition my condition was in.*

One of my family jobs is to be the caretaker of the house and grounds. At this time we lived on an acre of land in the rural suburbs. Our home's HVAC unit was located in a small storage pantry off the garage, and it was my job to change the A/C filters on a regular basis. One day during a period dominated by my intense work focus I had the thought, *"I better check the filters in the h/vac."* I opened the door to the storage pantry and looked at the masking tape I placed across the filter box marked with the date I last changed the filters. **I had not changed the filter in 2 years!!** HUMMM, I couldn't believe I had lost track of that much time! *Time flies when you're obsessively giving every ounce of energy to a mission from God.* **I had lost track of God's rhythms: *"evening and morning..."*. My body and my emotions had suffered.**

Life Coach Notes:
From the perspective I've gained in retirement, I have been able to appreciate the natural flow of life from one day to the next *as being an organic process of constant possibility that is always in development.* During all those working years, my perception could only have intellectually identified that we move from day to day, event to event, and goal to goal, but for me **to sense the flow from evening to morning and the grace in which that might transpire was not possible.** My mind seemed to focus on becoming better at what I did, or moving people from one level of spiritual development to a more effective level. *I don't remember feeling like I was participating in a flow of life and time, as it paced smoothly from "evening until morning."* **Instead** I was moving from project to project, meeting to meeting, special event to special event, and church season to church season. I have learned It is so valuable to follow intentional patterns which bring clarity to how our experiences flow from *evening to morning and morning to evening*, and thus provide us a chance to actually **rest into the flow**.

And that leads me to words 76 and 77 of Genesis Chapter 1.

Genesis 1:1-5 : "When God began to create heaven and earth and the earth then was welter and waste and darkness over the deep and God's breath hovering over the waters, God said, "Let there be LIGHT." And there was Light. And God saw the light, that it was good, and God divided the light from the darkness. And God called the light Day, and the darkness He called Night. And it was evening and it was morning, first day.

The term "first day" here is not preceded by the definite article **"the"** like in **"the first day"**. Translator Alter points out that *"the"* precedes the number of the day **only** on *"the sixth day."* **So, what's the big deal?** Translator Alter shares an observation about the translation which reveals a wonderful gift of his translation skill. The unique manner the Hebrews used in telling their story reflects their consciousness around the cumulative value of the **DAYS** of creation. He points out that in the statement, **"first day"** that finishes the sentence, the term *first* **in this and also in the 4 other "days" is used by the Hebrew author as a** *cardinal, not an ordinal, number.*

Honestly, I didn't understand the significance of that, and needed to spend some time with my dictionary **before I began to *get it*.** This **"first"** in the last sentence of the story is a **number denoting *quantity*** [one, two, three, of...] and **not a number denoting *the day's position* in a sequence.** *"The cardinality of a finite set is a natural number:* **the number of elements in the set."** [Check your dictionary.] It is a statement that in the **"set" of 6 days**, this is *first day* of six. **It is not the most or least important.** It is just **first** of **six. It does not have an exceptional status,** *it has an important position in a set.*

This is the big deal: Conceiving of the ***whole set of the days of creation as a complete unit with each unit being of equal value and totally inter-dependent within the whole*** is for me the most significant message and implication here!

Life Coach Note:
In this story every UNIT or Day of creation adds its gifts! The same manner in which your life adds gifts to all of creation. *Especially WHEN you find a WAY to live your most uniquely authentic life.* While you are not the first or MOST important *person within the whole of humanity, you are an essential addition that completes and enhances the WHOLE. You are so valuable in your uniqueness, and THAT* is how **God's WAY is revealed in history.**

"When one tugs at a single thing in nature, he finds it attached to the rest of the world."
"There is not a fragment in all nature, for every relative fragment of one thing is a full harmonious unity in itself." **John Muir,** Naturalist and "Father of the National Parks"

Every part of an ecosystem is in its own way essential to the health of the whole. BECAUSE **that is the way creation is constructed.** I believe those ancient Jews telling these stories had an intuitive sense of that truth even if they didn't have the rational science or frame of mind to back it up. They were sensitive to the WAY of God.

AUTHOR'S REFLECTION:
Putting things together.
So **Heaven and Earth are created** using every first, second, third, fourth, fifth, and *the sixth* **DAY**. *God begins all things in time* by **first** encountering **the earth then** as a void empty pile of *welter and waste*, with a punch list of differed maintenance items beyond counting or naming. Then the Great Creator God **brings forth a vision with a stated goal and intent** *to create heaven and earth from all that is not yet.* The **Divine Intentional Lover of All Creation**, and *envisioner* **of all that is possible** *speaks*, and in *speaking* **LETS-ALLOWS** all things to be made manifest; **to come into being**, and to add each unique gift **to the whole** through a time-line of evening and morning, evening and morning, evening and morning. *And here we are...*

Like this story about discovering the meaning and implications in the first 77 words of Genesis, there is so much more to learn and experience in the Genesis stories to follow. I hope to discover what the story tellers, *beyond any certain proof*, may have valued, intended, or just become aware of *by paying attention to their lives and telling stories*. This process helps me search my imagination for an aspect of my human experience on earth that might be informed and redeemed by a story's intention and meaning.

My guidance is to engage my perception, understanding, education, experience, and intuition, with the potential meaning discerned from some aspect of the Bible story. **I ask what it might hold for me *in hope* that I may better *understand God, myself*, or the relationships I have *with God, myself, and the world*.** That process brings the stories of Genesis into being relevant *living stories* as *current as your life or mine* while we discover meaning together within *the hovering breath of God* while attending Planet Earth University.

Ever forward!

Grace and Peace,
Phil Ball

Phil Ball

ABOUT THE AUTHOR

Phil Ball was born in Lawton, Oklahoma. After graduating from Candler School of Theology at Emory University in Atlanta, Georgia with a MDiv, he returned to Oklahoma to be ordained and Elder in the United Methodist Church, and began a 50 year career in Christian ministry through the United Methodist Church, and later in the Christian Church (Disciples of Christ).

In the fall and spring of 2018-19 he went through a nine month training as a life coach where he realized that he had finally *found his people.* His training affirmed his approach to sermons and teaching scriptures which had always been with the mind and heart of a life coach.

Phil's love of the ancient Hebrew scriptures, especially those of in Genesis, has provided much inspiration for him in both understanding and explaining God's amazing love & unwavering partnership with every person in every situation.

Phil retired from professional ministry in June of 2019, and continues to coach select individuals navigating life's challenges.

Made in the USA
Middletown, DE
24 August 2022